P9-CRA-297

Computer Security

PETER HAMILTON

First Edition

AUERBACH®
publishers

philadelphia
new york
london

AUERBACH Publishers Inc.,
Philadelphia, Pa., 1973

First published in Great Britain 1972

© Peter Hamilton 1972

ISBN : 0–87769–160–6

LC : 72–11766

Library of Congress Cataloging in Publication Data

Hamilton, Peter, 1917–
    Computer security.

    Bibliography: p.
    1. Electronic data processing departments—Security
measures. I. Title.
HF5548.2.H362   658.4'7   72–11766
ISBN 0–87769–160–6

Computer Security

To
Diana and Georgina

Computer systems are *not* secure and it will take much time and money before they are.

T. Vincent Learson,
Chairman, IBM
(Speaking in 1972)

Contents

Acknowledgements

My first debt of gratitude is to Willie Park, formerly of International Nickel and now with Decca. He is a computer expert and, more than anyone else, has helped me to understand the workings and terminology of that phenomenon. He has read every chapter and his comments and corrections have been indispensable to the completion of the work. Neither he nor anyone else who has helped me is to be blamed for any errors there may be. The responsibility is mine.

So far as I know, this is the first book of its kind. Like any pioneering effort it is bound to be imperfect and controversial. My hope is that some of those who read it will be good enough either to write to me with their criticisms or to voice them in other ways in the security and computer professions. The object must be to develop a correct philosophy and practice of computer security. I am sure that everybody accepts the need for this.

When the text was nearly complete I learnt that James Martin of IBM was engaged on a book to be published in 1973, which will be entitled *Security, Accuracy and Privacy in Computer Systems.* I have met Mr. Martin and he was kind enough to let me see his manuscript. It is clear that his book will make a valuable contribution to the subject. He is a computer expert, and his book is written mainly from this point of view. It is to be hoped that there will be a complementary gain by comparing the views of a computer man on security and of a security man on computers.

Next, I would like to thank my parent company of Chubb for all the knowledge, know-how and wisdom about security on which I have been able to draw throughout my working life with them. Although the writing of this book was a private task, I nevertheless felt it right to obtain permission of the chief executive, Mr. William E. Randall, DFC, AFC, managing director of Chubb & Son Limited. I thank him for his understanding and co-operation, but it must be clearly stated that Chubb should not be held responsible for any of the views or opinions expressed.

I should also like to pay tribute to the British Security Industry Association, of which I was honorary secretary in 1967–71, and particularly for the honour they paid me in making me their first honorary member. Under the wise leadership of their chairman, Sir Philip Margetson, KCVO, MC (also chairman of Securicor), and vice-chairman, Mr. Leonard W. Dunham (also deputy chairman of Chubb), the BSIA has achieved its principal objective of uniting the industry so that it may serve the national interest. I also acknowledge the help of BSIA's now autonomous offshoot, the National Supervisory Council for Intruder Alarms, and its director-general, Rear-Admiral Desmond N. Callaghan, CB. From all these I have learned much and am deeply grateful.

The following friends and colleagues have been kind enough to read the text for me and make valuable suggestions, or have helped by providing research material: my present chief and former comrade-at-arms, Dick Chapman, Bob Alderton of Chubb, Dr. R. L. Carter of Nottingham University, Norman Hamilton, director of Preslanders PR Services, Gordon Hasler, Roy King, computer services manager, Brunel University, Graeme Laws of Peter Bloomfield & Co., Victor Liardet of Chubb, Gary Marx, professor of sociology at Harvard University, Adrian Norman of the Inter-Bank Research Organisation and joint author with James Martin of *The Computer Society*, Robert Thomson and his wife Eleanor (Robert kindly read both manuscript and page proofs for me), and Mike West of Chubb, Canada.

The British Computer Society have been helpful to my researches and I am grateful to their secretary-general, Michael Ashill, for providing information and for making useful suggestions.

I have been fortunate in enjoying the friendship of members of the Institute of Criminology at Cambridge University. Professor Sir Leon Radzinowicz, who until recently was director of the institute and is known the world over as a criminologist, has been particularly kind and helpful, as have members of his staff.

I had the honour to be consulted by Professor R. V. Jones about his paper entitled 'Some Threats of Technology to Privacy' before he delivered it. I thank him for his permission to make extensive use of it in this book.

During my industrial security career I have had the good fortune to meet and make friends with many police officers from whom I have learned much. One of the more notable of these is chief superintendent Peter Marshall, formerly head of crime prevention at Scotland Yard.

This is the second book of mine that Tom Dalby has published. I congratulate him on his tolerance, and once again thank him for his friendship and wisdom.

Finally I come to the secretarial contribution, and my thanks are due to my secretary, Diana Milton; she has devoted much of her spare time to typing and retyping several chapters and to reading the manuscript. My wife, Patricia, has been, as always, the main prop of my strength and morale. She has also typed the bulk of the book, been my favourite critic and put up with the inconvenience, disturbance and neglect which the writing of a book inevitably entails.

Foreword

Security is a highly emotive word: its meaning can change with the context in which it is used; link the word with computers and one can set up a chain-reaction which leads, like a fuse, to the highly explosive ingredients of personal liberty and freedom. Who is secure today from the analytical maw of the computer and who knows for certain that personal data will not be mis-applied?

In this first book on computer security, Peter Hamilton has grasped the nettle, danger, and, through detailed research and gathering of facts, has moved some way towards the flower, safety. He has analysed the facts, interpreted the findings and made recommendations which, so far as humanly possible in an imperfect world, strike a balance between the security of a computer installation and the importance of the individual.

Many security measures imply a loss of freedom or an assumption of authority which it might well be argued on a philosophic, if not political, plane is antipathetic to the society in which we live. The line is sometimes dangerously blurred, for example between genuine marketing research and industrial espionage, and between legitimate industrial action and subversion. The choice is not an easy one to make but is nevertheless one which every management concerned with protecting the interests of their company in the widest possible sense must make.

Thus, in considering computer security, it is necessary for the professionals of the computer world, for management of computer-using firms and, indeed, for those on the receiving end of computer activity to weigh all aspects of the problem and the possible solutions. Sheer professionalism or inter-disciplinary knowledge will not solve problems of this nature. It will take men of sensibility and sensitivity, able to see the whole picture and the implications of each move and countermove, to arrive at the correct balance.

There has certainly been no shortage of books on either security or computers but until now there has been nothing to guide the manager on the problems involved in computer security, in appraising the risk of computer 'leaks' in terms of money, safety, political and social stability and identifying security risk-points and methods. This book therefore must be welcomed by all concerned with computers because it will alert them to aspects of computer risk probably never previously considered by them, and, of equal importance, the enormous cost of failure to anticipate any security breach.

The book is thoroughly practical and the checklist in Chapter 8, if meticulously followed, will at once reveal security weaknesses and indicate methods of overcoming them without prejudice to our free society.

Aubrey Wilson

Introduction

When a salesman from one of the computer manufacturers explains to his prospect the advantages in efficiency and economy of installing a computer, he seldom, if ever, refers to the security cost. Yet it is likely that the cost of protection of a computer system, in the corrupt and violent society to which we belong, will diminish or even outweigh some or all of the postulated advantages. In the future it may be that the main reason for using computers will not be efficiency or economy, but because the work that they do cannot be done by human resources in the time available; people may even have lost the ability or the will to do certain types of essential work.

Computers can be compared to nuclear physics in their impact on society. Both bring great advantages if they are applied to correct ends; if they are not, either can bring us to the brink of Armageddon or beyond. Just as the danger from nuclear weapons stems from enormous concentration of destructive power, so too it is the concentrative characteristic of computers that creates the main threat. This is particularly so of the larger installations which are being used to control industrial and power complexes 'on line'.

Concentration of any form of power or knowledge can be dangerous. The exercise of that power can be wrongly orientated, or its loss a disaster. A modern democracy with its many checks and balances and means of expression cannot easily be taken over subversively. A computer-controlled society could probably be taken over in a single operation in a matter of minutes—for example by a trade union to which all computer personnel belonged, or were compelled to belong on the closed-shop principle. When the homes of England were lighted by candles or oil and warmed by indigenous wood, its people could not be deprived of these essentials at a stroke by passive or active sabotage. Today, a walkout by comparatively few workers can deprive us of electric power, making it impossible to keep our economy at full strength and difficult to sustain life. A few emerging nations in the Persian Gulf or Mediterranean can and have threatened to deprive Europe of oil which might have similar effects on the lives and prosperity of 300 million people.

The computer is analogous to the human brain in its memory, calculating and control functions. But it is bigger, quicker and more accurate. Therefore its loss or damage or subversion would have correspondingly greater effects. If we take the case of a business that depends on the memory, calculating, collative and retrieval abilities of a hundred men, we can say that such a business would be difficult to bring to a halt; it is unlikely that more than one or two would be lost by illness or transfer at any one time and the business could undoubtedly carry on without them. It would also be difficult, if not impossible, to subvert more than a few of these, and such subversion would probably become apparent quickly. But the effect of the loss of the computer which replaces them would be devastating, as would its subversion, which might not be detected until it was too late.

It is tempting to speculate what would happen in future times if significant numbers of computers were destroyed and could not be replaced in a reasonable time. To what extent would society have lost the ability to carry out their functions? If one playwright is to be believed—and he made a convincing case—we are heading for a vicarious society. Certainly it is possible that visual and audio entertainment and teaching media may develop to a point where reading becomes unnecessary; in future generations this ability may be confined to scholars who need it for research.

Much public anxiety has been expressed about protecting people and their private lives from computers. This book concentrates on protecting computers from people which, until computers develop initiative, is the real threat. It also emphasises the physical and personnel aspects of security rather than the more specialised possibilities of misuse of systems design and programming, applications programming and direct operational abuses. The greatest danger posed by people mis-using computers is not intrusion into privacy, nor fraud nor industrial espionage, but subversion—the overthrow of democracy.

CHAPTER 1

Computers and Trends in Crime and Fire

Today's computer is intellectually a moron, and morally permissive. Provided it is instructed in a language it understands and is programmed to receive the instruction, it will do as it is told whether this be right or wrong. Not knowing the difference between right and wrong is its intellectual failing. Its immorality is that it does not care, and can make no effort to cure itself.

It is irritating to have to describe the computer in human terms as if it were a being, but there seems no other way to determine the nature of the security problem. Unlike man, it has—so far as we know—no original sin. Sin can be programmed into both. The relationship between man and subordinate man is similar to that between man and computer; and of course computers can be used to create and influence other computers. Man is largely an information process: so is a computer system.

The computer's first characteristic of interest to security men is the inhuman speed and scale of its operation. It can literally do in a few seconds work that would take thousands of men hours, days or weeks. It would be almost impossible to involve a thousand employees in major crime, but the computer needs only to be criminally instructed by one man to have the criminal capabilities of thousands.

This would not matter in a comparatively crime-free society. If the general affluence of our western society had driven out crime in accordance with the beliefs of some nineteenth-century philosophers, we could contemplate the future of computers with equanimity.

Thus the first tasks are to try to forecast the likely trends in crime in the future, and to estimate the risk of deliberate and accidental fire. It is the combination of the environmental and inherent risks which at once indicate and justify the security measures to be applied to computers.

B

The Present State of Crime

In an age when most people are better off, it is reasonable to expect a reduction in crime, especially crime against property. But the statistics prove otherwise. Currently over a million pounds a day in cash or goods is being stolen in the United Kingdom alone[1]; in the United States it may be four or five times that figure, and some estimates are higher even than that, probably because they try to take into account Cosa Nostra activities.

The total UK losses from crime are now running at £500 million annually[2], and with fire losses slightly in excess of this there is an annual wastage rate of more than £1,000 million, or about two per cent of the gross national product. Both have an important influence on the cost of living. Destruction by fire is irreversible and must be paid for; although some of what is stolen remains in the community, the thief increases his spending power without having contributed any real work. Moreover the owner of the goods has to be compensated for his loss by insurance or, if not, he budgets for loss and thereby puts up the price of his goods.

A particularly unpleasant feature of UK criminal statistics is that crimes of violence are increasing at a higher rate than any other. Leaving out the special case of Northern Ireland, crimes of violence in England and Wales rose in 1971 by 14·5 per cent[3].

All this is factual, but not necessarily indicative of a gloomy future. It may be that the trend will be reversed. Increasing affluence, and the greatly increased spending on social security measures, will, it can be argued, combine to eliminate poverty, hitherto thought to be a main cause of crime, and at the same time more widespread and costly education will correct the moral decline indicated by the present state of crime. The development of automation will result in the elimination of dull jobs and there will be more leisure; perhaps a four-day working week. Final steps in the emancipation of women will bring to bear in ever-growing force the influence of the gentler sex in the conduct of our affairs. Thus will the risk of computers being used for criminal purposes decline, not increase.

[1] The police-recorded figures are about £70 million per annum but these relate to known crime. The 'dark figure' is mainly made up by pilferage (mostly employee dishonesty) and evasions, and at least one government spokesman has confirmed that the true annual figure is nearer £500 million and possibly above it.
[2] Fire Protection Association (see page 114).
[3] Home Office Press Release, 29th March 1972.

And certainly it is important to try and gauge the future trends. First it is proposed to examine briefly the impact of affluence upon crime.

Crime and Affluence

At the beginning of the century there were only three crimes a year for every thousand people. By 1971 there were three for every one hundred—ten times as many[4]. The growth has continued since the First World War, but there always seemed to be some social evil to explain it. It was hoped that, with peace and prosperity, crime could be checked, if not reversed.

There has been no total war since 1945 and western societies have generally enjoyed a degree of prosperity hitherto unknown in the world. In Britain in 1969 there were 100,000 more crimes than in 1968[5]. Property offences accounted for most of the increase.

The eminent criminologist, Professor Sir Leon Radzinowicz, said recently, 'What is indisputable is that higher levels of crime are an inevitable reflex of affluence[1]. He went on to say that prosperity, not poverty, was directly related to crime figures.

A further indicator of the association between crime and affluence is to be found in the spending on social security. In the United Kingdom this rose from £1,976 million in 1964 to £3,538 million in 1970—about an 80 per cent increase[2]. During the same period the number of indictable offences rose from 1 million to 1·5 million—a 50 per cent increase. It is hard to escape the conclusion that, although much suffering may have been relieved, such a vast sum of money did nothing to increase the morality of society, which it surely would have done if there had been any connection between poverty and crime.

So much for the present and present trends. What about the citizens of the future; will they reverse them?

Crime and Youth

At a time when education has never been so widespread, when there have never been so many universities, when an enormous proportion of the national wealth of western societies is spent on education, it is disappointing to record that in both Britain and the USA there

[4] Sir Leon Radzinowicz (see page 115).
[5] Central Statistical Office.

has been a marked increase in criminal activity among the young.

In Britain there was only a small increase in the population from 54 to 55·7 million between 1964 and 1970, but the number of students in higher education went up from 239,000 to 427,000—nearly double[6]. In the same period, expenditure on education rose from £1,393 million to £2,513 million[6]—again nearly double, although some of the increase may be accounted for by cost-of-living rises. Yet today the under-21s account for two out of every three known burglars and three out of every five robbers[7]. In 1964 96,000 of the under-21s were found guilty at magistrates' courts of indictable offences, while by 1970 this had risen to nearly 140,000. At superior courts—assizes and quarter sessions the figures rose from 6,000 to 12,000[8].

It may be that there has not been time for modern mass education to make our society more moral, or it may be that educationalists generally do not accept current morality as an end of education.

Other impressionistic evidence suggests that indiscipline in schools and universities is getting rapidly worse. Stories of violence, sit-ins, strikes (the art of which British schoolchildren may have learned from their teachers as well as their parents), and other revolutionary activity are becoming more frequent. Such incidents as attacks by Cambridge University students, egged on, it would seem, by some dons, on the Garden House Hotel were particularly sensational, but their impact today is lost because of the frequency of acts of indiscipline on the campus.

The findings of Dr. W. A. Belson[9] of the Survey Research Centre of London University tend to confirm these impressions. After a most carefully conducted search using specially developed techniques, he obtained the following admissions from a sample of London male schoolchildren aged between 13 and 16:

I have kept something I have found	97%
I have stolen something belonging to a school	63%
I have stolen money	51%

No one is in a better position to know the British situation than the Home Secretary (then Mr. Reginald Maudling). He said in early 1972, 'I do not think the ultimate basis for law and order rests with the government, the law, or the courts. It rests on the family tradition

[6] Central Statistical Office.
[7] Radzinowicz.
[8] Criminal Statistics 1964 and 1970, H.M. Stationery Office.
[9] See bibliography, page 113.

and system. If the moral authority of parents is weakened, as in many ways it has been, the guidance they give their children diminishes.' He added, 'We are seeing a growth in the rate of crime which is disturbing—particularly among teenagers.'

The foregoing evidence and impressions have not been assembled to make political points, nor are they intended as moral judgments. They are quoted solely for the purpose of estimating security counter-measures.

New Forms and Methods of Crime

In 1970 the British Prime Minister, Mr. Edward Heath, forecast that the problem of the 'seventies was more likely to be civil war than war. Certainly there are many indications that our western civilisation is more likely to be destroyed by crime and fire than by nuclear war. Apart from the situation of Northern Ireland, which it must be remembered is crime, not war, Britain has experienced attempts on the lives of cabinet ministers and the former commissioner of police for the metropolis, and attempts to blow up important buildings. Powerful trade unions, whose methods of obtaining wage increases have been likened by one cabinet minister to blackmail, have ruthlessly pursued sectional ends without regard to the public interest.

They have developed new methods of hurting the public. For example, striking miners picketed power stations and nearly forced the closure of the entire electricity supply of the United Kingdom in 1972. Probably their action was illegal; it was certainly crippling in the social sense. It may be that trade unions have outlived their original purpose and that present hard attitudes and methods of obtaining rewards, indicate a need for a change in role.

Peter Drucker[10], the American management expert, has suggested that the western nations are at last leaving the social phase known as the industrial society. This does not mean that industry will suddenly cease to be a major factor in our lives. Drucker discerns a trend by which the industrial society, carried as it has been on the shoulders of the semi-skilled and unskilled worker, will soon become dependent on the men and women of knowledge.

There is already much reduction of drudgery in life, but the new style requires a new type—the technician, the technologist, the designer, the programmer. The disposal of the resulting mass of

[10] See page 113.

redundant workers is a problem mainly beyond the scope of this book, but not entirely; some of the known threats to computers have been to blow them up because they would cause redundancy. Moreover, the metamorphosis of trade unions will be prolonged over a number of years and is likely to be a painful period for western society. During this period there is almost bound to be some resort to force, if only of the mindless destruction type. Brute force still counts as a means of obtaining a reward, and our computerised, automated, electronic society will be highly vulnerable to it.

The pattern of crime will always reflect the social scene. In the welfare state we already know of criminal pension schemes, organised prison rescue operations, care of wives and relations of criminals who have failed. In this age of technology many criminals use sophisticated cutting techniques on safes and strongrooms. They design burglar alarm bridging devices and have used shortwave radio for control of operations and warning systems employing correct radio telephone procedures.

No doubt crime of the future will also reflect the development of Drucker's new society which he calls the knowledge society. In 1971, fraud cases in England and Wales showed an increase of 12·9 per cent[11]. In the United States fraud is already the most important form of crime, and incidentally is just about the most difficult to combat. At least robbery with violence and thefts of cash are self-announcing, but fraud may not be discovered for years. Fraud also requires a higher type of intelligence than robbery or burglary, and it would be a brave man who suggested that higher intelligences were more moral and less vulnerable to temptation.

The indications are that in the future we can expect greatly increased white-collar crime. There may be a consequential down-turn in violence associated with theft, although there is no sign of this yet. Such a down-turn might be more than offset by violence arising out of the activities of that new phenomenon, the urban guerilla.

In many parts of the world today groups of discontented or dis-satisfied persons have deliberately chosen physical and mental violence as a means of achieving their political and economic ends, in preference to the negotiating table, the court of law, or the ballot box. They range from the Tupamaros guerillas of Uruguay to the

---

[11] Home Office Press Release, 29th March 1972. Since going to press it has been announced that fraud cases increased by 30 per cent in the first six months of 1972 in London.

IRA; from powerful trade unions hurting innocent members of the public to the 'Weathermen'[12] of the United States; from groups of militant children to racists; from aggressive women's 'liberationists' to The Angry Brigade[13]. Whether we like it or not, these assassins, kidnappers, arsonists, saboteurs, blackmailers, hijackers, or whatever, exist in our western society and show signs of increasing activity, strength and pervasiveness.

Although the computer is in its early days, it has already been the subject of various forms of attack. Some of the attempts to destroy computers have been because they were seen either as symbols of automation, and therefore perhaps unemployment, others because they represent authority, any form of which is resented by large sections of youth; for example, students destroyed a North American university's computer centre. Other students cleaned the information off one thousand reels of tape belonging to a well-known chemical organisation (a thousand reels of tape could hold the entire details of the last British census). The Angry Brigade tried to blow up the police computer at Tintagel House, London[14]. Espionage against the BOAC computer is said to have deprived them of their marked lead in airline seat reservations[15]. Encyclopaedia Britannica had their customer files copied from their computer and sold to a rival[15]. Forte's were defrauded of over £43,000 by one man feeding fraudulent information into their computer[16].

As we become more dependent on computers, it can be expected that they will increasingly be a target of attack or misuse. One form of threat to computers comes from a recently-formed organisation known as Computer Professionals for Peace, which has its headquarters in Brooklyn, New York[14]. The CPP has expressed beliefs that institutions and industries who use their computer to support, directly or indirectly, the United States defence effort should be

[12] A terrorist organisation which is attempting to destroy American society by discrediting the reputation and destroying the morale of the forces of law and order. One of the leaders expressed their philosophy as follows 'Every trash we do, every bomb we plant, is forcing The Man (the system) to repress. . . . He has to buy more pigs (policemen) and more machines and the taxes go up and the people get screwed even more. . . . We are costing The Man money and we make him paranoid. . . . Twenty pigs hit already. . . . Every pig is looking over his shoulder, they go round in twos and threes. They can't get recruits.' (*The Guardian*, 26–28th October 1970).
[13] A revolutionary organisation in Great Britain which made attempts on the lives and families of government ministers and carried out various bombings.
[14] *Industrial Security*, August 1971.
[15] *Security Gazette*, January 1972.
[16] *Security Gazette*, January 1972.

neutralised by its local members refusing to participate in the national defence effort. The CPP is actively soliciting membership from the computer professionals and technicians throughout the USA, and some reports indicate the existence of a similar organisation in the United Kingdom.

Accidental and Malicious Fire

In an age when fire prevention and fire extinction measures have been highly developed and are backed up by strict legislation in many parts of the world, and when wood has to a large extent been discarded as a building material in favour of virtually non-inflammable concrete, one would expect the fire picture to be brighter. It is. There is more flame than ever before. In the United Kingdom the fire losses in 1957 were £22 million and there were five hundred fatal casualties. Today they are approximately £130 million and fatal casualties are running at about one thousand a year[17].

But these figures do not tell the whole story since they represent the direct losses only. If the indirect losses, such as forfeited orders, penalty clauses for uncompleted contracts, labour drift, permanent change of customer habit, were taken into account the grand total of fire damage could be estimated at more than £500 million.

It seems that the basic causes of fire increases are the growing complexity of industrial and domestic processes, especially the increased use of electricity, and an attitude of mind, which also affects crime, of not really caring. The vulgarism 'couldn't care less' accurately describes a pervasive attitude to property. Each year security fire guards find tens of thousands of acts of carelessness such as burning cigarettes in waste-paper baskets which, if not discovered, could have caused major fires.

Most disturbing of all is the fact that it is no longer possible to assume that fire is accidental. Arson has shown a marked increase. Rather over ten per cent of large fires (damage of £10,000 or over) were due to malicious causes, according to the Fire Protection Association, in 1970[17].

The proportion of damage due to malicious causes was more like 15 per cent; this increased damage is probably due to the fact that fires started deliberately are likely to cause greater damage. Moreover,

[17] Fire Protection Association—see page 114.

it is thought that a number of fires in the 'doubtful origin' category were, in fact, malicious.

On high risks it is now advisable to couple fire detection and protection with defence against unlawful intrusion, and also against externally-mounted arson such as throwing petrol bombs or other incendiary devices from the street.

There have been a number of serious fires affecting computers, and their vulnerability to fire is well illustrated by the fact that two of the more notable computer fires have occurred in the premises of computer manufacturers. In one case the loss was over £2 million. Brief accounts of some of the fires have been published by the Fire Protection Association[18].

Why Has Crime Prevention Failed?

When it is so obvious that crime is reaching a dangerous height, it seems strange that no really drastic measures have been taken by the authorities responsible. One answer is wrong preventive policy. Government and the police have tended to support the view that the probability of detection is the best deterrent. This may well be true where organised crime is concerned. Large, sophisticated operations will probably not be defeated by purely defensive means, and a powerful and centralised CID may well provide the best answer to the activities of gangs such as those of the Richardsons and Krays.

But the big gangs are not the only problem, nor indeed the main problem, which is that unfortunately we live in a mass thieving society. This is not the place to make a detailed examination of the causes, except insofar as they give guidance to the degree of protection which must be applied to computers. The following three causes, it is suggested, may contribute to an understanding of the security measures which will be recommended later.

Titillation of appetites. There can be no doubt in anybody's mind that display and advertising foster, and are intended to foster, the strongest possible desire to have the goods in question. Obviously in many cases they are beyond the reach of people's pockets, and so tremendous temptation is created.

Changing disciplines and loyalties. There has without doubt been a demolition of disciplines and restraints over the past 50 years which

18 See page 114.

formerly had helped people to resist temptation. It has resulted in permissiveness, which, being translated, means the assumption of the right to please oneself, regardless of its effect on others.

Abundance. There has been an enormous increase in the actual amount of property. Together with the facility of cheap insurance, this has resulted in carelessness about property which as previously mentioned, also contributes to fire incidence.

The numbers of people nowadays engaged in crime against property in one form or another cannot be calculated, but a pointer comes from the researches of the Cambridge criminologists, McClintock and Avison[19]. They have calculated that, on the basis of existing crime in the UK, 8 per cent of women and 31 per cent of men will be convicted of a standard list offence (which includes indictable and certain non-indictable, but serious, offences) at some time during their lives. It should be remarked that this estimate does not include motoring offences except for a few very serious ones. This may mean that about a third of the population has been, is, or will be engaged in crime.

It is not very difficult to see that the detection of such a large number of criminals presents very serious problems. If we can assume a detection rate of 40 per cent of recorded crime, this becomes insignificant as a deterrent when recorded crime is probably no more than one-quarter only of the total crime committed. Yet how often have senior police officers made statements such as the following: 'The certainty of detection is the best deterrent'? This could only be valid if there were such a thing as certainty of detection. It is in fact an appallingly weak argument, based as it is upon an unrealised and unrealisable premise. Almost all detection occurs after the fact, and this, coupled with the incredible rise in crime, negates detection as a serious deterrent in conditions of mass thieving. If the detection theory had been valid, surely it would have manifested itself by now in reduced crime.

It is only fair to add that this point is accepted by the bulk of modern police officers. The new Commissioner of Police for the Metropolis of London, Mr. Robert Mark, began his tenure of office by breaking the central control of the CID and subordinating it to divisional commanders. It is to be hoped that this heralds a return to the precept of the first Commissioners of the Metropolitan Police,

[19] See page 115.

Richard Mayne and Charles Rowan, stated in 1829 and which cannot be too often repeated: 'The principal object (of the Metropolitan Police) . . . is the prevention of crime. To this great end every effort of the police is to be directed. The security of persons and property, the preservation of public tranquillity, and all the other objects of a police establishment will thus be better effected than by the detection and punishment of the offender after he has succeeded in committing the crime.'

The foundation of the prevention of crime against property is care by the owner, who in most cases today is a corporation. Security of property is therefore the responsibility of management or householder, mainly management.

At first sight it seems strange that management does so little about security. Why do so many managements prefer to budget for loss or insure against it rather than prevent it? One reason given recently by the head of a well-known supermarket chain was that if he did not lose three to four per cent of his turnover by pilfering and shoplifting, he sacked his display manager. He may have been exaggerating to prove a point, but the fact is that the national loss on turnover is about one per cent, and it is likely that many companies are losing more than this. They may forget that a loss of one per cent on turnover often means 20 per cent loss on profit, and that to replace one stolen article at cost it is usually necessary to sell four more. Surely, too, management has social responsibilities which it ignores at its peril.

The answer is that to be effective, security, whether against fire or theft, has to be ahead of the risk, but it is very difficult to persuade a cost-conscious manager to pay for expensive equipment against a risk which has not materialised. He will, of course, buy equipment after the event: after the old-fashioned safe has been defeated he will buy a modern one. But there are other consequences of the defeat of the old safe. There is a sequence of events not unlike the industrial picture of many western countries today where rising wages chase rising prices, resulting in more rising prices. The sequence is as follows:

Out-of-date or non-existent security
Successful crime
Organised crime becomes capitalised, mass petty thieving whets appetites

The cost of living rises because losses have to be paid for in
  higher prices and increased insurance costs
Security costs rise through increased wages and increased
  criminal competence and numbers
Prices rise again

The root of the problem is patchwork security. Reduced to its
simplest terms, this is the pattern:

A householder has his front door opened and property stolen
  by a burglar because he has only a simple latch lock
He therefore buys a mortice lock
A second burglar comes through the back door and so a mortice
  lock is fitted to that, too
A third burglar opens the windows, so the householder buys
  window-locks
His claims experience is now so bad that he cannot get insurance
  unless he fits a burglar alarm

And so the story goes on. It may sound exaggerated, but it is
meant to illustrate a faulty approach to security. It will be noticed
that nothing happens in advance of the crime. The householder
always waits until it has been committed. As a hole in the defences
appears, a new piece is put in. Each new piece represents the failure
of the previous one.

A general impression of computer security in this country indicates
that patchwork security is once more being applied.

.   .   .   .   .

In addition to the indications provided by statistics, the conditions
which can now be associated with widespread crime, that is, affluence
and permissiveness, are almost certain to continue. The computer,
whose security is the subject of this book, together with automation
are, in general bound to create greater affluence except in the unlikely
event of total war. Probably the consequential unemployment problem would be overcome by greater leisure. It is only surmise, but
greater leisure may itself provide a nursery for crime by reason of
boredom and lack of challenge.

Who can doubt that we are far from seeing the end of permissiveness? The increasing domination of militant women's organisations
and the militancy of children, both suggest further breakdown of

family life and the pursuit by a ruthless and violent means of selfish sectional ends at the expense of the community.

Thus the computer age begins in a climate of massive and increasing crime. This is the backcloth to the examination of the computer's vulnerability to attack and the conclusions and recommendations about its security which follow.

CHAPTER 2

The Vulnerability of Computers

A computer system consists of the following main parts:

Hardware. This term describes the computer itself, i.e., the central processing unit, its backing store, and its peripheral equipment; *viz.*, input and output media used for translating plain into computer language and *vice versa.*

Data is the input information which the program processes to produce output information, and also describes the contents of the stores.

Software describes the stored programs of the computer and is of two main types:

    (a) Systems software or programs. These are programs provided by the manufacturers which automate the handling of the machine.

    (b) Applications software. The problem-solving programs developed by the user to suit his business requirements.

Data bank. This consists of the stored history or current information of the enterprise. In most concerns its most recent information is constantly used for reference purposes and as a basis for future operations.

Communications. These are the landlines and the associated apparatus which permit remote use of the computer. In large enterprises there may be a hundred or more remote terminals through which information can be fed into the main computer, or extracted from it. Nowadays in many cases visual display units (VDUS) are connected to the main computer so that managers and others concerned can have immediate and visual access to information.

There are two major types of electronic computer—digital and analogue. The latter are less versatile and not much used in business;

therefore the term computer in this book refers to the digital variety. Even the digital computer can perform only five functions:

> accept and store information;
> move information from one place to another within itself;
> perform arithmetical operations on numerical data stored in memory;
> compare two pieces of information in memory and say whether they are equal or not, or positive or negative, zero or non-zero;
> write, punch out, or display the stored information.

At first glance these functions do not appear to be particularly impressive, and in fact the computer's true importance lies in three main characteristics. It carries out these functions on an incredibly large scale at incredible speeds and with incredible accuracy.

Within industry computers have two broad applications: to provide technical control information and management operating information. In its application the computer has a variety of uses, but the most important are the solving of mathematical problems and control of dials or processes. Generally, technical information systems require no management judgment; since the data and the answers are absolute, management's decision-making role is probably confined here to deciding whether to use a computer and, if so, what kind, in just the same way as management approval is required for the purchase of a new piece of scientific or engineering equipment.

In its other main business application of processing non-technical information for use in decision-making, its role is far less precise and certainly does not, in the end, obviate the need for risk-taking, or management flair. It can, however, reduce the risk element by its ability to process information speedily, accurately and in great quantity.

Vulnerability Theory

Vulnerability is a technical term used in security to indicate the amount and type of protection which ought to be given to particular assets. It is usually expressed in two stages: general and specific. The general vulnerability is determined by consideration of the following:

1. *Physical characteristics.* The question to be asked here is, what adverse things can be done to the property that will injure or

deprive its owner? For example, money can be stolen, a house destroyed, an employee subverted. These are straightforward examples, but there are some more difficult. A valuable painting can be stolen, but it may be unmarketable because it is too well known, and therefore this aspect of its vulnerability low; on the other hand, it is easily destroyed by accident or malicious fire, or by water or explosion.

But sheer value alone can make property vulnerable—a variation on the precept that all men have their price. Even more far-reaching factors, such as inaccessibility, mobility, indestructibility, may enter calculations, but these are irrelevant to the present study.

2. *Scale and nature of hostile forces.* If, as we must suppose in remote Utopia, no one wanted to steal, destroy, or damage the asset concerned, there would be no point in protecting it (except against accident); however valuable, its vulnerability would be minimal. This is the extreme case, adduced to ensure realism in security planning, which must be related to the threat posed by criminal or other hostile activity or conditions.

3. *Dependence.* An item of property may be physically invulnerable, or have no vulnerability because there is no criminal activity, yet it may be vital to a company's or a nation's survival; so much so that its loss or severe damage, even from accidental causes, may be fatal. Alternatively, and more likely, there may be so little criminal activity and the property only mildly physically vulnerable, yet so much dependence is placed upon it that it has to be protected as if it were highly vulnerable for other reasons.

An example is an island dependent on electric power supplied by one power station. There is no known threat to the power station from any enemy, and it is not easily destroyed. But the dependence of the islanders on it for their life and safety make it so vital that it has to be given the highest degree of protection. The highest form of protection known, incidentally, includes the provision of alternatives.

4. *Replacement capability.* Some security theorists include this as part of the dependence factor. When vital equipment can be replaced within a reasonable time if destroyed, they argue, dependence is reduced. But this ignores cost of replacement and other

costs, such as lost production, unfulfilled orders, change of customer habit, labour drift. Moreover, separate consideration ensures that the factor is not overlooked when security is planned.

Specific Vulnerability of Computers

If the vulnerability theory is applied specifically to computers, it is obvious that they are highly vulnerable on the first two counts. They are fragile, valuable, subvertible, and they operate in a climate of high criminal activity and incidence of fire. Dependence on them varies, but there can be as much as 90 per cent of a company's vital information and computing ability at risk. Usually, too, they are only economic if they do carry and process a high proportion of the company's information.

It has been estimated that within five years all important industrial and commercial information will be computerised, and additionally it can be asserted that a large proportion of the more complex industrial processes will be controlled and monitored by computer.

It is possible that by the early 1980s, by a combination of technological necessity and menial reluctance, we shall be largely, if not totally, dependent on computers for our way of life.

For replacement purposes, hardware and software must be separately discussed. Hardware can be replaced, but as a general rule the more expensive it is, the longer the replacement time (and, one may assume, the greater the dependence). Software cannot generally be replaced, and this can mean considerable delays in reprogramming alone. The data bank would for practical purposes be irreplaceable.

Replacement capability is adversely affected by—
incompatibility between the hardware 'architecture' of the various manufacturers, and individual manufacturers' ranges;
incompatibility of programming systems or languages;
incompatibility of operating systems used;
incompatibility of peripheral equipment.

The construction of the main frame of the computer takes almost a year, and since the frames are mainly assembled from equipment supplied by other manufacturers (OEM—original equipment manufacturer), the knock-out of a single component manufacturer may affect several computer manufacturers. Usually remote back-up

C

facilities are arranged, but these are largely honoured in the breach and are, of course, themselves subvertible.

Total destruction of the vital parts of a computer system, that is, the computer itself and its associated data bank, is not the only hazard, nor necessarily the worst, that its owner faces. The following paragraphs examine other hazards in each phase of the system's development and operation.

1. *Systems design.* This is determined by the requirement, e.g., business computation or process control. At first glance there seems little scope for ordinary criminal activity, but it is conceivable that a system could be designed to be responsive to malpractice at a later stage. For example, a spying capability might be built in without the knowledge of the customer's programmers, or indeed any other part of his management team. This need not necessarily be done by the insertion of an eavesdropping device. (In fact, this has already been tried by a national intelligence agency.)

   Using once again the human analogy, the systems design corresponds to the design of the brain which determines, for example, whether a man shall have the capability of an accountant, an engineer, or a philosopher.

2. *Programming.* To carry on the analogy, the programmer's job is to ensure that the engineer, or other brain, is 'trained' to its particular function; e.g., production. Programming is intended to express the management will as determined by system design, or produce collated information in particular contexts. Here substantial opportunities for malpractice are evident. A computer can be programmed to pay money to companies or individuals to whom money is not owed. Its program may be manipulated to give wrong answers to particular problems to facilitate fraud, or to give wrong information whose application would damage the company and assist competitors.

   That branch of programming known as systems programming, which deals with the operating system or software supplied by the manufacturers, provides for the automatic reporting of 'halts' or 'interrupts' as part of the computer control system; in other words, the danger signals. If these can be subversively manipulated, malpractices may continue undetected for a time due to the suppression of entries in the computer log, which is maintained automatically.

3. *Data input.* Here once again it would seem that almost unlimited opportunites for malpractice exist. Data input is the day-to-day updating of the information as products are sold, or as external conditions alter. Wrong data, which would result in a wrong management picture, can be fed in, as can unauthorised invoices, to take advantage of previously fraudulent programming.

Data usually have to be transcribed from plain English into machine-readable form as punched cards or tape, magnetic tape, or other media described as data carriers. If these should include standard prepared forms or documents; e.g., cash dispenser cards, then manipulation or decoding of these presents a further hazard.

4. The *data bank* is the store of the recent and past activities of the company. In the event of a disaster to the computer and its software, and provided other computer facilities were available, the company could get back into business reasonably quickly on the basis of its data bank. If the data bank were destroyed, this possibility would be lost and so, in most cases, would be the entire records of the company—its accounts, its debtors, its creditors, its know-how. In the case of a company with 90 per cent of its records computerised, it is doubtful if it would be viable after total destruction of its data bank.

5. *Communications—terminals and landlines.* Computers are now designed to serve outstations of an industrial or commercial complex direct. In other words, it is no longer necessary to supply data for the computer by post or telephone and receive data similarly, but it may be done direct over permanent landlines, private or public, from outstation to computer headquarters. The same considerations about input and output discussed above apply, but new possibilities arise of a highly complex technical nature—electronic interception and eavesdropping. The risk of information being stolen is increased by VDUs which are susceptible to unauthorised use and observation.

The use of terminals and data transmission lines to make possible time-sharing on large systems opens up a whole new world of security risks in the use of passwords and codes. The rapid development of *en clair* visual display units in industrial and commercial undertakings constitutes about the highest risk to management information yet.

The vulnerability of computers may be summed up as follows:

accidental or deliberate destruction of or damage to hardware, software and data carriers;

perverted systems design;

perverted programming;

false input data, including via terminal;

misapplication and theft of information from the computer, from the data bank, through the terminals, or by observation of the VDUs;

electronic interception of communications.

Security has the capability to defeat all these threats provided that it is incorporated as part of the management function. (*vide* chapter 7—Computer Security and Risk Management).

CHAPTER 3

Relating Security Theory to Computer Vulnerability

Security began neither as an art nor a science, but as an instinct, and it is fundamental to an understanding of the subject that this is realised from the outset. Man's greatest concern throughout his history has been with security—the security of himself, his family, his possessions and his way of life. Security is, in fact, a survival discipline, invented by nature to ensure the continuation of the species, and it is most highly developed in mammals.

The most important manifestation of mammalian security consciousness was the care of its young. While vegetable life ensured its survival by the random method of profligacy, and other animal life risked the external hatching of its eggs, mammals nurtured their young in the mobile fortress of the womb, and enlisted the aid of the male as a guard and commissary. While other living beings left their offspring exposed to the dangers of cold and heat and the attention of wild beasts, the mammals, especially man, kept their young with them while they were too weak to fight their enemies and taught them the arts of survival. The apprenticeship's lengthening as life became more complex made the partnership of man and woman an enduring one, which gave rise to man's finest institution, marriage, whose purpose is now, as it was originally, security.

Man soon learned to give depth to the defence of his family, by hiding his wife and his children in a hollow tree or behind some heavy rocks, especially at night. Later caves were used with boulders for doors, and the site was carefully chosen so as to be difficult to find and to attack without making a noise. Like many animals, early man liked to jabber and he soon found that he could use this noise to warn his family or his friends when danger threatened. A particular noise meant tigers, another elephants, and so on. The human voice was thus the first burglar alarm; security was probably the origin of language.

The rigours of early existence, and especially of the glacial period, which threatened to destroy the human race, taught man that he must provide against disaster. Soon he learned to store food, in case of famine, animal skins and fuel for fire against extreme cold. Later there were communal stores for use in emergency. This was, of course, insurance—which is the concept of communal responsibility for individual loss.

Security, like any other discipline, has now become susceptible to technology, but the fact remains that no one, however skilled, devoted or well-paid, can look after another person's property or life as well as that person. Being largely a defensive technique, it requires maximum incentive to make it work. This brings us to a first principle of security, but before it is stated some general remarks about the principles of security must be made.

Although security today is a science as well as an instinct, it is, like economics, a practical one and thus the principles which guide its various branches are not scientific laws, whose observance produces a definite result, nor are they like the rules of a game, failure to comply with which brings a certain penalty. The principles of security illustrate methods and ideas which have been successful in many cases, and in general they provide sure foundations for the establishment of a security system. Ignorance or disregard of them is apt to be dangerous and will often be unnecessarily expensive in time and money.

It is very difficult to decide any order of priority for the main principles of security applicable to owners of computers. Those postulated below are all equally important. The order in which they are placed reflects an approach to the subject rather than their relative significance.

First principle: Protection of assets is in the first place the responsibility of the owner. This is equally true of human assets, although it cannot be expressed in this way. The board of directors of a company as the shareholders' representatives have, or should have, the maximum interest in safeguarding the human and material assets of that company.

If one states this proposition in public, indignant citizens invariably rise and say that these things are the responsibility of the police. This is nonsense. Except in the case of a definite threat to particular property or life, such as may be posed during a strike or industrial dispute, which may involve both 'insiders' and 'outsiders', it is not the task of the police to give specific protection to individuals or their property. The task of the police is to ensure as far as possible the general maintenance of law and order. There are not many policemen, and it is most important that these competent and highly trained men should not be bogged down in static guards, but should be mobile and flexible, and thus able to concentrate at the threatened point when required.

There is, however, a limitation on what the owners of property or those responsible for the safety of their workpeople can be expected to do. They are not expected to defeat armed attack, although the measures they take may delay such attack. Force has to be met with force, and the defeat of a military-type attack is a military or police responsibility. Measures taken by the owner are therefore complementary to the role of the police and, if necessary, military forces.

In no area is this principle more valid than that of the protection of computer systems. Their vulnerability to many forms of attack, such as explosive or incendiary bomb throwing from the site perimeter, directed either against the computer itself or its supporting service plant; e.g., air-conditioning or stabilised power supply, and the increasing dependence which industry has on them should induce the greatest concern for security on the part of the board responsible.

Security of the type available to the owner is no weakling, and applied scientifically and in accordance with these principles it can often be decisive in itself. But being essentially defensive, it is only truly effective in the context of close support from other sources of which, of course, the police is the primary one.

Security arranged and controlled by the owner with the assistance and skill of the security industry has the following intrinsic capabilities: it can control access to the target and to the vicinity of the target; it can alert the defences and summon help when an attack takes place or is imminent; it can do much to ensure the loyalty of persons having legitimate access to the target. The branch of management concerned with the implementation of this principle is called risk management.

The second principle arises from the limitations of defensive measures. These make it imperative that there is close liaison and first class communications with the police, whose technical and human resources and power to concentrate at the threatened point are highly relevant to him.

Second principle: Close relations with the police will increase the strength of the owner's protective system. Every police force in the United Kingdom has a crime prevention branch, whose officers can give skilled and impartial advice to managers on the best methods of protecting their assets. They will indicate security equipment and services which have been found to be reliable. Perhaps most important of all, the police force throughout the country can respond, often in a matter of minutes, to alarm calls from threatened points.

Police advice and alarm response capability are highly relevant in the case of bomb attacks on computers, for they either have, or have quick access to, bomb disposal resources.

A corollary of immense importance to this is that the more efficient property owners' total security measures are, the better the police response will be. Fewer false alarm calls and less petty theft mean fewer wasted police man-hours; the police are thus able to concentrate on really serious crime and violence.

Security is an expensive matter, and once security measures have been decided upon it is is usually advisable to concentrate the risks as much as possible so that such money as is spent will be used to maximum effect. This also means that irksome restrictions affecting the free movement of employees and visitors are as limited as possible.

In the case of the computer, the concentration of the risk has already taken place, often to an extent to which all the eggs are in one basket. In situations such as this security, since no way has yet been found to make it absolute, insists on the provision of alternatives. When the government considers the security of the state, it classifies various installations in grades which indicate the dependence of the nation upon them. The top grade consists of key points whose loss or severe damage would be disastrous to the nation. Government security men faced with the task of securing such a key point insist on the provision of an alternative. No government security man would ever allow that the control of the population in time of emergency should be dependent on one broadcasting station, or that the country's electricity supply should derive from one immense power station, or even that power stations should be dependent on one kind of fuel.

The next principle, therefore, in relation to computers may be stated as follows—

Third principle: Where the loss of or severe damage to the computer system would be disastrous to the company, alternative means must be provided (and regularly tested or checked). The assessment of the degree of disaster which would arise from the loss of or severe damage to a company's computer can only be carried out by the company concerned, but this assessment must be made.

It may be postulated that a dependence of less than 70 per cent would probably make a computer system uneconomic. A company which on security grounds refused to commit itself to more than 50 per cent dependence would probably become uncompetitive against a company which allowed its dependence to go up to, say, 90 per cent or more. It seems a reasonable assumption that those companies which were reluctant to allow a high dependence on the computer would inevitably be dragged lemming-like towards the 100 per cent dependence point.

If it were a practical proposition, the next principle would therefore be that total dependence requires total security, but it is not, and an attempt to reach a 99 per cent state of protection would be in the same cost area as having a standby computer permanently idle. A firm taking either course would be uncompetitive unless all others in the field did the same, in which case mankind's progress would be greatly, perhaps fatally, retarded. Clearly the practical alternative step is to arrange to buy or borrow computer time. Equally clearly, this must be planned in advance. If no contractual arrangement can be made, several alternatives should be sought. So much for the computer itself.

Of the remainder of the system, software, data and data banks are vulnerable to severe damage, subversion, theft or destruction. Thus master files and transaction files must certainly be duplicated, for their destruction in the case of 70 per cent dependence or more would almost certainly be disastrous. Such duplication in remote, secure storage would almost certainly be a condition of fire and consequential loss insurance.

Here, then, alternatives under the direct control of the management concerned are practical and reasonable in cost.

The mere fact that alternatives can be arranged does not in any way lessen the need for security. Alternatives for the computer itself are, as we have seen, not wholly satisfactory; nor is the loss of the original to be courted on financial grounds alone. And similarly the provision of duplicate input, output and file data does not lessen the need for safeguarding the original—the duplicate data will never be quite up to date and the switch to another computer service or duplicate data, in the event of the original data being destroyed, or the computer put out of action, will at best be an unprofitable hiatus.

It is arguable that the duplicate data need not have so high a degree of security as the original, and where countermeasures against destruction by fire or sabotage are concerned, this is true. But it must be remembered that these are not the only threats. Duplicate data might have a high value to a competitor, as would the know-how which could be obtained from computer systems specifications and application programs, and the very fact that money has been spent on providing a duplicate system justifies reasonable safeguards.

To sum up so far, it is argued that in theory a reasonable degree of flexibility may be achieved by the planned provision of alternative computer facilities and by the duplication of computer records.

The best alternative plan can only be second best, and its existence must not be allowed to detract from the exceptionally high degree of security which must be provided in the working environment. And the first important principle in the achievement of this may be stated as follows:

Fourth principle: The criterion of access is need. The first application of this principle is concerned with denying by physical means physical access to the vulnerable point or its immediate vicinity to any person who is not authorised to be there.

Not only should regular access be confined to those who have a duty to go into the computer environment, but these persons should be as few in number as possible. A conscious effort must be made to reduce staff to an absolute minimum, even if this means, as it may, that senior personnel may have to perform a few menial and maintenance tasks. Menial tasks in a high security area are not menial at all, and can be performed only by highly responsible people. Moreover, it is not enough to control access to the computer room or other vulnerable parts; it is also necessary to control access to their vicinities. To get near the perimeter of the computer room itself, or immediately above or below it, is half the battle for the illegal intruder who wants to place bombs or slip in unnoticed. And the same is true of data banks and terminals and communications, although there are obvious limitations to the supervision of landlines, only a small part of which will normally come under the control of the computer's owner.

The word access has a second and technical meaning in computer terminology in that it is used (both as a noun and a verb) to mean electronic entry to the system for the purpose of obtaining or implanting information. Thus care must be taken to distinguish between physical access and electronic if there is any possibility of confusion. This fourth principle covers, and is intended to cover, both types of access.

Unauthorised electronic intrusion can be prevented to some extent by physical means by the owner, but since access can be gained to his systems at places outside his direct control; e.g., by intercepting landlines or at telephone exchanges, his means of control is reduced to detection and the creating of electronic barriers by the use of codes.

Seniority itself does not convey an automatic right to access. Need, not rank, is the criterion, and managing directors and other senior executives must set an example.

Right of access on grounds of essential duty must be confined to the relevant times. Persons who have a duty to enter the computer environment should be prevented from using their right of access at times when their duties do not require them to be there.

With all the modern means available, such as card access control systems, which are discussed in the next chapter, it is possible to achieve almost perfect control of access. Its efficacy depends entirely on the validity of the authorisation systems, and this is the job of personnel security.

.   .   .   .   .

The power of computers, the likely dependence on them not merely of companies, but of a society, justify a radical approach to the problem of personnel security. It is an axiom of security in a democracy that security measures must defer to the concept of human freedom. It is for this reason that Gestapo-like methods, man-traps, poison gases and other repressive and lethal forms of protection, may not be used in security, and in any case they are eventually self-defeating. Security, after all, is designed to protect a way of life, not to change it. What is the use of achieving near-perfect security if the way of life it was intended to protect is thereby destroyed?

Having said all this, there are circumstances in which some infringement of liberty is justified. The Security Service, the police, the armed services, certain government appointments, must clearly in many cases be subject to special rules of conduct which infringe their civil liberties. Background enquiries through the use of police records and other confidential information, special regulations and high standards of personal behaviour and conduct must be accepted as necessary in the interests of the state.

Of course, security measures such as these are negative, as their purpose is to eliminate untrustworthiness rather than to create loyalty, and they are unlikely by themselves to be successful. Positive measures to give pride in the job as well as material incentives are an important part of security.

If the requisite degree of security is to be created in a computer environment—and it must be remembered that police records are not available for commercial and industrial security purposes—then something more than conventional personnel measures must be considered. Unless this point is accepted, the computer cannot be secured, which, it has been argued, could permit disaster to a company or, *in extremis,* the overthrow of a political system.

The only known security device which enables men and women to remain loyal to their jobs under great stress and temptation is high morale—a sense of being different, of public responsibility, of belief in the task or cause. This is what sustains soldiers under fire and doctors and nurses under stress, and makes them put others first.

Therefore the final principle which it is proposed to adduce may be stated as follows:

Fifth principle: An essential complement to the highest possible degree of physical security for computer systems is to ensure that regular access to the system and its environment is permitted only to a specially created élite.

CHAPTER 4

Physical Security and Control of Access

In terms of correct architecture and design, physical security, whose main purpose is to control access, is simple, cheap and efficient. The phases in our history in which some attempt has been made to incorporate reasonable security at the design stage of buildings are few, and for this the architectural profession must bear some blame. The ages of castles and caves are among them, but certainly for over a hundred years or more contemporary architecture appears to the security man to have been based on the supposition of a dawning Utopia. Therefore in many cases today physical security is complicated, expensive and, if not inefficient, at least not as efficient as it should be, which is a major factor in the current crime explosion.

Computer systems are no exception to the general rule of anti-security design. This particularly applies to their siting. Among favourite positions is the base of a multi-storey building. Each bomb threat—these are fairly frequent against computers—requires the evacuation of the building. One computer is sited immediately adjacent to the packing area of a large industrial concern, which is also the area of maximum fire risk.

There is no doubt that (from a security point of view) wrong siting of computers will continue for some time, since in many cases they will be added to existing commercial and industrial complexes and inevitably 'fitted in somewhere'. For this reason, and because computers vary in size from desk-top models to those requiring large buildings to house them, the security manager or adviser can only state the ideal and make the best of what he gets.

In these circumstances it is neither practicable nor desirable to give detailed specifications for construction or equipment; that is the job of the architect, construction engineer and security consultant working together on and hired for the particular job. The ideas and recommendations which follow therefore indicate what should be done, rather than exactly how it should be done. Those who feel that some of these are excessive should remember that a computer system can represent an investment of £4 million or more, and perhaps look again at Chapter 1. Obviously the security of smaller or less valuable installations must be tailored accordingly.

Siting

The best possible site for a computer complex would be an isolated one. The more remote a site is and the less cover available, the easier it is to control access. Flat, wide open, unpopulated spaces make identification of authorised and unauthorised persons simple. It is unnerving for someone who has no business in a particular installation to have to cross such a space, especially if he or she is carrying weapons or explosives or incendiary materials.

This psychology was well known to dictators like Mussolini, who used an elongated office for his audiences. After entering the door, visitors had a long walk under the gaze of this formidable man, which gave him the initiative.

It cannot be stressed too strongly that security at its best is not a purely defensive art; security men are always looking for means to restore the initiative to the defence. Thus from the moment that the decision is taken to have a computer, the security man must do his best to ensure remote siting, be this within the industrial complex or in an entirely different part of the country. There is no technical need for the management computer to be either at head office or the works, but if it has to be at either it must be physically separate, and this particularly applies to above and below. Process control computers will usually of necessity be within the works or laboratory complex.

Another consideration in the siting of a computer centre includes the selection of an area likely to be free from civil disturbance. In view of the increasing turmoil on the campus and the evidence that computers are a target for dissident students, it will usually be desirable to site a computer well away from educational institutions. At the same time, in accord with the élitist concept[1], the area ought to be attractive residentially to the computer technicians and the professional men and women who must be closely associated with it.

Computer centres should also be sited away from areas liable to flooding and, of course, away from high fire risk areas.

[1] See page 38.

Obviously similar considerations apply to satellite installations, but here in most cases the siting is almost certain to be within some other complex and isolation has to be achieved more by physical construction than by geographical placing. This is a weakness, and it will be suggested in more detail later that it may be overcome or greatly reduced by the establishment in the main computer complex of a security monitoring unit.

Construction

Central and local government laws and regulations will affect some construction plans. Since these laws will vary from place to place, the recommendations below may not be realisable in some cases. Security-conscious architects will be able to devise suitable alternatives.

The material of which a computer centre is built should have as its chief characteristics high resistance to fire and impact. If wood has to be used as part of the construction, it must be subjected to fire-retardant treatment. If possible there should be no opening windows, or, better still, there should be no windows at all. Light should be provided artificially or, if permanently closed windows are used, the glass must be toughened to an extent comparable with the strength of the walls, supported by external grilles grouted into the walls. If civil disturbance is a threat, it may be advisable to provide special emergency steel shutters which can be electrically operated.

Ventilation should be artificial and this, of course, suits the computer itself, which requires special ventilation. The air-conditioning system should be entirely self-contained and not linked to any other area; ducting for this and smoke ventilating systems must be grilled at regular intervals, as must cable channels. There should be no external access to ventilation systems or insurgents may be able to introduce noxious or toxic gases.

Preferably there should be a reserve system of ventilation but, if not, replacement parts for critical points of the system should be available within the centre. If there is any likelihood of long periods of electricity cuts, alternative supplies should be available within the computer centre, not only for the purpose of keeping the electronic equipment in operation, but also to maintain air-conditioning.

Most important of all, there should be only one door for regular access. Any other doors required for fire escape purposes should be kept to the legal minimum, and it should not be possible to open them from the outside. Internal keys should be kept behind break-glass panels.

Fire brigades will advise in detail as to the exact requirements of the law and their officials may well recommend the use of push-bar escape doors. Security-wise these are bad because an illegal intruder who has managed to evade other checks may be able to make a quick getaway.

It may be that single or multiple reinforced concrete pillars would be the ideal base for a computer complex. This is favoured by some banks in the USA for strongrooms. But it would be necessary to ensure that the area underneath did not form a tamping area for sabotage (explosives in trucks, for example), or facilitate arson (parked petrol tankers).

The data bank could be similarly constructed on separate pillars adjacent to pillars bearing the computer.

Control of Constant and Regular Access

Correct siting and construction will have made access control as simple as possible. The object is to prevent, detect and act against illegal intrusion, whether by force or stealth, of any unauthorised person or materials, and it is equally concerned with ingress and egress.

Access control is highly vulnerable to blanket or perpetual authorities to enter. The heads of Britain's security services have always refused to have any form of blanket or permanent pass for themselves, and have insisted on going through the normal visitor's procedures when entering vital and vulnerable installations.

Authorisations to enter a given vulnerable point should always state the hours at which authorisation is permitted (and, if appropriate, the days of the week). They should be for a limited term, certainly not exceeding one year. Authorised persons arriving or leaving at unusual times should be regarded with suspicion. The right of search of persons and their possessions by authorised searchers should be a condition of employment. The right should be used with discretion and searchers must be of a specially sympathetic disposition.

Apart from controlling the main entry point, security can be further enhanced by dividing the controlled area into security compartments, usually called keeps, to which access according to need can be maintained. Only in a few cases should it be necessary to give particular persons right of access to all keeps. The natural divisions of a computer centre are:

A Data receipt and distribution area (data control section)
B The library for tapes, discs and program cards
C The operation area around the computer

If *C* is the most vulnerable and vital part of the centre, then security would be enhanced by restricting access to as few people as possible.

The exercising of access control in its simplest form is by a guard who recognises the person applying for admission and knows him or her to be authorised, but human beings are not only fallible, corruptible, often lazy: they are also, today, extremely expensive. The modern tendency is to control access by electronic means.

One system involves the use of a punched card coupled with a numerical code. The card, which is personal to the holder, is inserted into the locking device. The holder then taps his own personal numerical code, which he has memorised, onto a keyboard. Control is therefore exercised by means of an electronic process—a simple form of computer. The great advantage of this system is that it does not respond merely to a key, but requires also an identification. To be a card holder is not enough.

The system has the following additional advantages:

(1) If a card is lost it can be programmed out of the system.
(2) The system can be so programmed that card holders may only enter and leave at their permitted hours.
(3) The system may be aligned with a keep system.
(4) All movement is recorded and may be checked by means of a print-out.
(5) If for some reason it suspects the identity of a card holder, a delaying device can operate and concurrently an alarm can be given.
(6) It can give an alert in the event of non-arrival of an expected person.
(7) It is highly flexible and can be applied not only to buildings, areas, doors, floors and keep systems, but also to filing systems.
(8) A fail-safe device can be built in to allow easy egress in the event of fire.

D

Strong doors, properly hung by hinges accessible from inside only, should be closed and opened (electronically) by high quality lever locks, operated by the card access control system. Ramming of an access point or other part of the computer housing by heavy impact, say of a lorry driven at speed, can be prevented by the erection of vertical reinforced concrete posts, rather like anti-tank barriers, in front of vulnerable parts. There is a Swiss pattern road-block which can remain hidden in the ground until actually needed.

It may be necessary to supplement the card system by some form of invigilation. This could conveniently be done from a security control unit[2]. This access system is of course being continuously developed by the security industry.

Occasional Access

So far, access control has been considered only in relation to those whose duties require constant and regular access to the computer complex. Unfortunately (from a security point of view) it will be necessary from time to time for others to enter the premises. Managers are naturally proud of their computer centres and will wish to show visitors round. Members of the board may also wish to pay occasional visits to an area of high investment. Service engineers, consultants, telephone engineers, fire brigade inspectors, managerial students, are among others who will require occasional access.

The first essential is that these visits must be kept to a minimum and once again it cannot be stressed too strongly that mere seniority, is not a passport to enter a security controlled area. Need, not rank, is the criterion of access.

The security procedures for those requiring occasional access should include the following:

(1) All visitors must be clearly identified as such, preferably by a lapel badge of distinctive colour and type. This will indicate to permanent staff the need for security in conversation and documents being worked on.

(2) Visitors should be escorted throughout the visit, either by security personnel or by an official of the permanent staff of the computer centre, and this also applies to visits to lavatories.

[2] See page 52.

(3) The identity and purpose of the visitor must be recorded in a log which should be of the card type. Visitors' books are not recommended because they may reveal to all who look at them the identities of other persons who have visited the centre. The card logging system referred to above can be adapted to record visitors in its memory.

(4) Visitors should not be allowed to bring overcoats, parcels, briefcases or other packages into the computer complex. (In one existing access control system, male visitors are required to remove their jackets as well as their overcoats and are then issued with a distinctive topcoat without pockets.)

(5) A visitors' pen or gallery may be useful.

Canteen

Unless they are working on a highly secret project there is no reason why computer centre staff should not make use of ordinary catering areas, in the works or head office if they are so located. Where the computer system is isolated, or where information security so demands catering facilities should be provided outside the heart of, but within, the computer complex. Catering staff change frequently and are therefore difficult to supervise from a security point of view; moreover, supplies have to be delivered by outside personnel. It is essential that catering facilities have no direct communication with the heart of the computer. This does not mean to say that security precautions should not be taken in the catering area. They must be, on grounds of information security alone.

Fire Protection of the Computer and Peripheral Equipment

The most important fire precaution is to prevent it ever happening. The first stage, therefore, is the elimination of hazards. If possible, smoking should be forbidden in computer rooms. Accumulations of inflammable material such as waste paper or celluloid must be avoided. Automatic waste systems have been developed in the United States by which waste material is put in a slot in special ducting and then sucked or conveyed by belt to a suitable point in the complex, where it can be pulped or shredded or incinerated (but this must be a low fire risk method). This is, of course, not only a fire precaution, but also good for security of information.

In cases in which very high information security is required, secret waste and all waste from secret areas should be shredded at point of origin before being conveyed to the point of final destruction.

If fires nevertheless occur, the earliest possible warning is required. Seconds, or even fractions thereof, can make a difference in the efficacy of extinction methods.

There are three forms of automatic detection which have application to computer centres.

(1) *Heat detectors.* There are two kinds—fixed-temperature detector which responds only to a predetermined temperature and rate-of-rise or compensating detector, which distinguishes between a slow rise and a fast rise in temperature. The latter has application to such things as machinery, which may gradually heat up but not be a fire risk as such. A rapid rise in temperature would, however, indicate that something was wrong. Fixed-temperature detectors have the advantage that they are generally simple and cheap, but they do tend to operate after a serious situation has occurred.

(2) *Smoke detectors.* These detect the products of pre-combustion processes and, generally speaking, give the earliest possible warning. They cannot, however, be used in places where the products of combustion might normally be present in the atmosphere, such as in a garage.

(3) *Radiation detectors.* Most flames emit infra-red and ultra-violet rays and many materials send out infra-red rays while they are heating, even before the wavelength reaches the display spectrum. Detection of these can be obtained by the use of special cells and the use of electronic amplification to operate an alarm.

In air-conditioned atmospheres and in electronic circuitry generally, smoke detectors tend to be the most reliable and to give the earliest warning. But specialist advice, either from the fire brigade or reputable industrial companies, is necessary to determine what type or combination of types of detector is applicable to particular circumstances.

Detection of fire is not sufficient by itself. Automatic communication of the alarm to all concerned by the quickest possible means enables the following operations to take place:

(1) Evacuation of threatened personnel to a safe area. If a drill can be evolved which facilitates the preservation of vital documents without prejudice to human life, so much the better.

(2) Local and immediate fire extinction facilities can be brought to bear.

(3) The summoning of the professional fire services, who will also be responsible for salvage.

Fire extinction within computer complexes is a difficult matter, since that prime extinguishing agent—water—cannot always be used without damage and danger. The most useful local extinction agent in computer rooms is carbon dioxide, which is effective in confined spaces. It does have to be used with extreme caution, since, although not toxic, CO_2 can cause suffocation or a slowing down of reactions. CO_2 systems can be triggered either manually or automatically, with a time delay factor to allow for evacuation. The efficient use of such systems depends on proper control in the event of an emergency. Emergency planning should ensure that endangered areas can quickly be evacuated, isolated, and then flooded with CO_2. An evacuated and damaged building must be guarded until sensitive information or valuable material can be removed or otherwise secured.

Fire Extinguishers

Portable fire extinguishers at strategic points are invaluable as first line extinction agents provided they are used in accordance with the manufacturer's instructions. Danger to life can arise if, for example, water extinguishers are used to control fires in live electrical machines, and they are worse than useless in controlling oil fires.

The following are the recommendations of the Fire Protection Association[3] for the use of fire extinguishers with computers and ancillary equipment.

Carbon dioxide or halogenated hydrocarbon extinguishers should be provided near the central processor and associated equipment, and the equipment should be designed so that the extinguishing agent from the extinguishers can be readily and safely injected.

[3] See page 114.

Water (gas pressure) or water (stored pressure) extinguishers should also be provided in the computer area near any equipment handling large quantities of paper.

Water (gas pressure) or water (stored pressure) extinguishers should be provided in or immediately outside rooms and vaults in which records are stored.

Safe Storage

It is not generally known that in recent years there have been considerable advances in the design and construction of safes specially designed to protect all forms of computer records and data. Since the loss of almost any records or data can cause at least an undesirable hiatus in operation, it is well worth evolving a system of storage which will take full advantage of modern equipment, and at the same time separate or reduce areas of concentration of risk.

In the first place, the amount of records kept within the computer area should be the absolute minimum required for efficient working, and regular checks and constant reviews should be made to ensure that this state is maintained. Such records which have to be kept in the computer room should be kept in a safe specially designed for the purpose.

The most important data kept in the computer room is in the backing store in the form of magnetic tape reels of various sizes, magnetic disc packs, magnetic drums or cassettes. If the irreducible minimum is contained in the computer room, these will all be 'on line' to the computer and therefore housed in cabinets designed and supplied by the computer manufacturers.

It appears to be general practice for this kind of storage to be of minimum protective value where resistance to fire and other hazards, such as demagnetisation, whether accidental or deliberate, are concerned. There appears to be need for research in this area and for a marriage of thought and action between the computer manufacturer and security equipment manufacturer.

If data carriers of whatever kind are stored in the computer room when not in operational use, then they must be housed in the best quality protective cabinets. These or their prototypes should have survived fire endurance and drop tests (the latter to simulate collapsing floors during fire) without significant damage to the structure of the cabinet, and without effect on the data within. As there is a number of inferior products on the market, the greatest care in selection is needed.

Similar considerations apply to records kept outside the computer area. As an alternative to safes, externally stored records can be kept in specially designed fire, heat and moisture resisting vaults, but as the possibility of theft may be a major consideration probably the best method is to store such records in safes of the type described, but within a burglar-resisting strongroom.

Generally speaking, materials which give protection to records against fire are vulnerable to determined attack by criminals, and *vice versa*. Although some safes with a high degree of resistance, both to fire and criminal attack, have been designed, it is better practice to separate the two operations as indicated above.

It has to be borne in mind that this data store, as these latter records are usually termed, constitutes the main means by which a company could recover in the event of total destruction or severe damage to its computer and peripheral equipment. Thus, however good its protection may be against fire and crime, it is usually unacceptable to depend utterly on it and some duplication of records is therefore essential. For the duplication, microfilm can reduce considerably the amount of storage space required for duplicates, and once again special record protection equipment is available.

Remote storage in safe and temperature-controlled vaults underground can be rented from at least one commercial firm specialising in this facility. In fact the retrieval system is sufficiently good for original historical data to be kept there if this is desired, but probably the duplicates would have in such a case to be kept elsewhere.

In this area of safe storage, as in so many other affecting computer protection, it is highly desirable to consult a commercial company as to the best storage arrangements for the particular computer operation. It should be remembered that humidity, steam and magnetism are often as dangerous to computer records as heat and fire.

Electronic Access Control

If there is multiple usage of a computer, there is immediately a major security problem. Computer service bureaux are greatly concerned with this and have developed what may be loosely described as locking systems, by which the various users can gain access to their rented information and computing facility by means of more or less elaborate codes and passwords.

One enthusiastic salesman of the services of a computer bureau compared his particular system to that of a safe deposit, which is a bank of little safes, usually with double locking systems, one key being kept by the renter and the other by the overall custodian. This is fallacious and even dangerous, because it gives the impression that a positive shut-out can be achieved, which is not the case. The break-in is essentially a cryptographic problem, and in any case a long book could be written about safe deposits that have yielded their treasures to the wrong people.

There is considerable discussion among computer experts as to the effectiveness of electronic locking devices.

The access problem of service bureaux is reproduced in large computer complexes with many terminals and long landline communications. Once again, electronic locking or selection may be useful, but probably the greatest deterrent and detector will be a security monitoring or control unit, of which more anon. Physical control of access points will also be a considerable aid, whether these be to bureaux or to the main computer complex.

Security Lighting of the Perimeter

Nearly all illegal intrusion takes place under the cover of darkness and then lighting is an important facet of defence. It is also a strong deterrent to the intruder and its power to deter varies directly with the skill in selection of the equipment, its siting and installation. These are complicated matters best left to an expert, who should insist among other things that the security lighting is:

> of sufficient intensity to enable the defence to discriminate between friend and foe;
> not patchy, nor leaving shadows for intruders to hide in;
> not dependent on any one source of power;
> the kind of light which accentuates contrasts of colour rather than blends them, as some very strong lights tend to do;
> not so positioned that it dazzles the defence.

An effective and economical method of using security lighting is to link it to intruder detection devices, so that initiating the latter switches on the former and illuminates the intruder, for whom this can be a frightening experience. He may be temporarily dazzled and demoralised, and will be vulnerable to a quick follow-up by guards and dogs, if these are part of the general defensive system.

Professional Advice

Professional advice on fire prevention, detection and extinction is vital for the following reasons:

almost every situation requires a tailor-made solution;

there are statutory requirements which alter fairly frequently:

substantial reductions in insurance premiums can be obtained by compliance with rules made by the insurance industry's Fire Offices Committee;

it is also important to reduce the fire risk in adjacent premises, and the fire brigade authorities can be helpful in this respect;

there may be consequential dangers, such as corrosive fumes given off by burning insulation, which need special and immediate remedies outside the scope of normal fire prevention.

Emergency Procedures

Management must as an inherent part of its function do its best to ensure the continued operation of the computer centre in the event of an emergency, whether resulting from civil disturbance or natural disaster. It is not enough to ensure correct siting and construction of a computer complex; these facilities must be used to their greatest advantage. If operations cannot be continued, for example, because of danger to personnel, then plans for an orderly evacuation must be the counterpart of automatic damage limitation measures.

As a minimum, an emergency plan should include the following:

(1) A communication channel to disseminate information and instructions to all personnel.
(2) A procedure for the immediate securing of all tapes, programmes, and other valuables.
(3) Designation of evacuation routes.
(4) Designation of wardens to take control.
(5) Primary and alternative transport and routes in the event that it becomes necessary to send employees home.
(6) Medical arrangements.
(7) Duplicated communications to police and fire brigades.

(8) Procedures to ensure the maintenance of vital accounting and research processes in the event of destruction of or severe damage to the computer. This usually means prior arrangements to buy or borrow computer time.

(9) Training and designation of replacements of key personnel who may be injured or killed.

(10) Security procedures to come into operation to cover the disruption period and to supervise the emergency arrangements for continuing the company's operation.

(11) A plan for salvage in the event of disaster. The importance of this is highlighted by a fire in the United States involving a computer and other equipment loaded on a furniture removal van. A quick salvage operation which cost a little more than $10,000 saved equipment worth $142,000.

Security Control Unit

Enough has been said to demonstrate the complexity of the security of computers. The growing dependence of major companies on their computers makes it mandatory to have a permanent and specialist security operation. Security of the type required is extremely difficult to achieve without a specialised approach, and it stands no chance of being effective unless it is supported by the great majority of those whom it affects. It will not be effective if it becomes a spy system, and its operations, however thorough, must be as open as possible and must be seen to be impartial and fair. For example, security personnel should be subject to all security procedures and should set the example in compliance and cooperation.

Its task in a computer complex should include the following:

(1) Preparation and revision of the main defence plan against fire and theft.

(2) Invigilation of local and technical access control.

(3) Searching.

(4) Manning of closed-circuit television monitors and surveillance generally (*see chapter 6*).

(5) Internal audit of computer operations.

(6) Background enquiries of men and women working in the computer complex and aftercare (*see chapter 5*).

(7) Interception of communications for monitoring and audit purposes.
(8) Inspections of security areas.
(9) Practising of security arrangements.
(10) Drawing up and testing of emergency plans.
(11) Liaison with police and fire services, commercial security companies and other external agencies concerned with security.
(12) Design and supervision of electronic locking devices.

Clearly the security man in charge must ensure that his various duties and tasks do not unduly hamper operations. Closest consultation with the manager of the computer complex is necessary.

. . . . .

The proper application of the precepts and practices advocated above will make it extremely difficult for an intruder to enter the computer complex by stealth or by force, or by remote technical means, and should limit fire or other damage by accidental or deliberate means. It will not defeat the authorised man or woman, who, for some reason or other, is or becomes of evil intent. That is the job of personnel security.

CHAPTER 5

Security of Computer Personnel— The Creation of an Elite and a Climate for Honesty

Physical security measures correctly designed, applied, and supervised can prevent the access of unauthorised persons to vital and vulnerable areas of a computer centre. Within the computer centre they can ensure segregation according to need. Physical security cannot however ensure the original or continuing loyalty and integrity of those whose duty it is to work in or visit regularly the computer centre and who are therefore authorised to do so. This chapter and part of the next are therefore concerned with the measures which can be taken to ensure that those who do have constant access to the centre are and remain pure in the security sense. They are only concerned with persons requiring constant and regular access. Those whose duties require them to have occasional access should be treated in exactly the same way as visitors (*see p. 44*).

It must be said at once that many of the recommendations and solutions to the problems which follow are to a greater or lesser degree intrusions into the privacy to which an individual in a democratic society is normally entitled. They also have the effect of creating a privileged class. The justification for these measures has already been argued in preceding chapters. What is wanted in a computer man is a deep sense of responsibility to fellow men and women.

The creation of such an élite in the past has had very little to do with money but, in the present rather material society, rates of pay are likely to have a greater significance. The security man cannot alter the society in which he lives and he must accept that today the positive incentive of extra money will be a real safeguard.

In addition to incentives to responsibility there must be very strong disincentives to disloyalty. These might be similar to the penalties which face medical practitioners who abuse their trusted position in society. Perhaps they should be even stronger. The government might encourage with all the means in their power short of legislation, the formation of a chartered society for computer personnel, expulsion from which should debar them for ever from access to computers. Clubs for computer personnel should be encouraged, but membership of certain trade unions may have to be discouraged.

For example, Mr. John Cousins said at a London seminar on 19th April 1971, 'We know as quickly as the employers about the state of their business.' Mr. Cousins is secretary of the public services and civil airports section of the Transport and General Workers' Union. He indicated that trade unionists employed on computer bookings of seats on airlines feed back to the unions information on long-range forecasts. Thus the unions can get a good idea of the future profits likely to be made and use this information in support of wage demands. But this may be a communications problem rather than a security one.

Militant labour organisations generally rely on accurate information of management plans so that disruption may be maximised. In addition, there are several research institutions, such as the Institute for Workers' Control[1] and the Labour Research Department (nothing to do with the Labour Party), which need managements' information for political purposes. Although there is no evidence that they practise industrial espionage, both are well-known collectors of industrial information.

Furthermore, passive sabotage on the lines of go-slows, work-to-rules, and strikes, should be regarded as totally unacceptable negotiating methods for computer personnel. Since it is the policy of some unions to use passive sabotage in vital industries such as power and transport to extort higher wages, there must be no intrusion of this kind into computers, where the possibility of blackmailing the community is infinitely greater.

The British Computer Society is making strenuous efforts to establish a computing profession, and this surely will eventually provide a basic protection for society. How realisable this aim may be is another matter. There have been notable efforts by the council and secretary general of the BCS to ensure that members accept and implement the highest standards of ethics. The principal tenets of the

[1] A full account of this organisation is given in *East-West Digest*, June 1972.

BCS code of conduct require that members will (1) accept full responsibility for any work undertaken; (2) behave at all times with integrity;
(3) act with complete discretion when entrusted with confidential
information; (4) act with strict impartiality when giving independent
advice.

If the members of the BCS accept and uphold the BCS code a
considerable safeguard will have been achieved. But, of course, the
influence of the BCS is limited to its members, and there is no requirement on owners of computers to employ BCS members. Its membership at the time of writing is rather more than 16,000 out of a possible
40,000. Its sanctions are therefore limited. Its rules do not limit
political activity nor does the membership form require background
details; e.g. criminal record, political affiliation.

Moreover, there are indications that some elements of the BCS
membership do not accept the need for codes of conduct or rules
about ethical behaviour. In an age when institutional, professional,
and national loyalties are being increasingly called into question by
the young it is arguable that a system of voluntary disciplines is
unworkable. Indeed, the BCS publication *Aims and Activities* makes
the following point: 'It may be that in the foreseeable future large
computer installations will have to be licensed, in the interests of
public welfare and private protection and legislation providing for
such licensing might have to extend to the personnel concerned. In
such a case the Society, with its professional structure and Code of
Conduct, could play an essential, leading role in the implementation
of controls.'

One may comment here that for the Society's hallmark to be
meaningful its selection procedure for admission to membership of
its various classes—fellow, member, licentiate, affiliate, associate, or
student—would have to be more thorough in the security sense than
is indicated by its proposal form at present. It is appreciated that there
would probably be considerable opposition from some elements of
the membership to any form of security filter.

It is clear that the BCS share some of the fears expressed in this
book. It may well be in the future that the BCS, with or without
statutory powers, will be able to some extent, to control the market
for computer personnel and that major companies will insist on the
hallmark of the BCS on their computer employees. Even so, the other
measures of personnel security must be employed as additional
safeguards. In the present time when there is no registration or

licensing of computer personnel, these other measures are of even greater importance.

Selection Procedures

All persons having or intended to have constant and regular access to the operational area of a computer centre or its communications, or any of its terminals, should be requested to submit to a background investigation. Refusal to so submit should be regarded as a decisive reason against employment in the centre.

Applicants should be told at the outset that there will be two interviews: one for technical reasons, that is to say, in connection with technical suitability for employment, and the other in regard to their security suitability. The latter interview should revolve round a special form to be completed by the applicant. The first question on this form should be to this effect: 'Do you agree to investigations being made into your background to establish the truth of what you have said in your application and your security reliability?'

Probably the technical application form will include a number of questions which are also relevant to security, but this does not mean that such questions should be omitted from the security questionnaire. On the contrary, it is not always easy to remember what lies one has told, and to have to repeat answers in separate interviews sometimes confuses amateur spies, of which there are plenty. This is the old hundred-question technique of interrogation, where a suspect is asked a hundred searching questions about himself and his background over a period of two or three hours or more. Then, when he thinks it is all over and relaxes, the same hundred questions are asked again. Both times the answers are recorded on tape. If he is a phoney or is being untruthful, this may be shown up by comparing the two tapes. (It is not suggested that this technique is necessary for interviews of the kind under discussion).

It is also important that there should be a suitable preamble, preferably on the form. This should explain and justify the security precautions, but its main object must be to set the security tone of the company. It must convey to the honest that the firm, while taking security seriously, is fair and understanding, and to the dishonest that its security procedures are thorough and continuous.

Security men of great experience, like policemen or customs men, may get a feel about people which, when taken in conjunction with

other more tangible indicators, may be useful. But there is no sub-
stitute at this stage for proper and systematic investigation of the
applicant's background. Each statement made in his application form
that can be verified, should be verified.

One of the many dodges used to secure employment is to use as
reference a fictitious company at the address of a friend or relation,
who replies in glowing terms either with or without a forged letter-
head. One false reference was written by someone purporting to be
the managing director of the firm concerned. He said he was writing
from his home address as he preferred to give all references personally
in his own handwriting. Unfortunately this got through the personnel
investigator; the applicant secured employment in a well-known
security company and did some damage to the reputation of that
company when it was discovered. The personnel investigator must
make it a rule not to accept references that cannot themselves be
verified; his tools include telephone directories, trade associations,
institutes, the directory of directors, and the telephone.

The firm should require a full list of previous employers and, of
course, gaps in employment must be accounted for. Whether there
has been previous employment or not, full educational details from
the age of twelve onwards should be required. In addition, all applicants should provide the names of two non-commercial or professional referees, e.g. head master, doctor, lawyer, chartered accountant, etc. all of whom can be checked from the appropriate register.

The political views and affiliations past and present of the applicant
are relevant to security. No posts of a security classification should
be given to extremists.

The fullest information about date and place of birth, names and
addresses of parents and spouse and spouse's family should be
required. Checks should be made by letter or by telephone, from
public records and, in some cases, by personal visits.

It will be appreciated that background checking is expensive in
both time and money.

Employers do not have access to criminal records and there has
recently been considerable agitation for them to be made available
in certain cases. It has been suggested, for example, that security
companies should be allowed to check their personnel against police
records. In fact, The British Security Industry Association[2] has never

[2] The trade association representing by volume of business about 90 per cent of the
British Security (against crime) industry. See page 113.

supported this view. The value of a check against public records is overrated, and more than balanced by the odium which such a step would arouse.

There would be a tendency to overvalue so-called 'police clearance.' With the detection rate of known crime running at something like 40 per cent and known crime thought to be no more than 20 per cent of the grand total, the chances of slipping through the net would be very good indeed. Moreover, any serious criminal or subversive political organisation would be unlikely to try and infiltrate someone with a police record.

A far better plan is to make one's own selection procedures as valid as possible and supplement them by aftercare. Additional protection will be obtained by obedience to principle number two[3] which enjoins the closest possible relationships with the police. After all, there are not usually more than thirty or so persons employed in major computer centres, and it is not difficult to allow a police contact to see the list of persons so employed. Knowing as he does the importance of computer centres, it seems unlikely that a responsible police officer would not take some suitable action if he discovered that someone with a bad criminal background was serving in one.

There is a vetting technique much used in Germany and increasingly in this country to ensure that personnel occupying positions of responsibility are free from serious character blemishes, and that round pegs are fitted into round holes. This is graphology. The study of handwriting in this country tends to be regarded as something on a level with astrology, but there is reliable evidence to show that it is a valuable aid to personnel selection which should not be overlooked in a security context. There is an excellent book on this subject by Noel Currer-Briggs and others[4].

Indoctrination and Personal Security

Indoctrination is the process of initiating a person in the responsibilities of secret work. When a person begins work in a computer centre, his or her security responsibilities should be clearly explained. This explanation may include the following:

any work which is of a particularly sensitive nature;

[3] See page 34.
[4] See page 113.

E

the names of colleagues with whom he may freely discuss his
work;

the relevant details of the security system, including the security
rules (it is often better to read these out rather than hand out
copies);

the consequences to the company and to him personally of a
breach of security. A major and deliberate breach of security
or repeated acts of security carelessness should disqualify a
person from future employment in a computer centre and
perhaps from membership of the BCS.

In addition, he must be trained in the art of being personally secure
and of setting a security example. He must scrupulously observe
security rules, however high or humble his position; be discreet in
his conversation with others who do not need to know about his work;
not expose himself to blackmail by personal irregularities and excesses;
be careful of his own office security. He should not leave important
data lying about. For short absences it may be sufficient to lock such
data in a strong drawer. For longer periods, they must be put in their
proper container.

Security pairing is a useful drill. In this, two colleagues in the same
work arrange to check each other's security. At close of business they
try each other's safe and files to see that they have been properly
locked, that papers have been put away, and so on. It is sound practice
never to close the door of a safe or the drawer of a file without
locking it.

Psychological Security

If the foregoing advice has been implemented, the personnel at the
computer centre will already be not only a technical élite, but also an
élite in the social sense. The security selection procedures and indoctrination should have made them feel a sense of responsibility
commensurate with the power of their position. But this will not last
long and will be a diminishing force against perversion and subversion
unless efforts are made to establish and maintain a state of high
morale.

The factors which will encourage a man or woman to stand firm
in the face of temptation to betray his organisation are spiritual,
moral, intellectual, and material. Spiritually a man must believe in

what he is doing. He must be enthusiastic about computers and feel that they are not only improving the performance of his firm, but the lot of mankind also. It follows that the company purpose must be one which he can believe in. He must know that his company is worthy of its task and that his leaders are worthy people and care about him. To him the company must represent the highest layer of current morality, whatever that may be at the time.

Intellectually he must have confidence that the leaders of the company know their job. Finally, and more important today than ever before, his conditions of work, including his salary and his pension, must be ones which in the sum will make him envied by others. It is important to realise that size of salary alone does not, and never will, produce and sustain a state of high morale.

The successful creation of an élite depends as much upon the external view of it as upon the internal psyche. It is essential that the computer centre and its personnel be looked up to, admired, respected by the rest of the corporate community. They should be held in the same esteem as good doctors or professors. This will not happen if computer personnel indulge in intellectual snobbery, assume airs of importance, or are pompous in their dealings with others.

A Climate for Honesty

It may be banal to say that it is all a matter of good leadership inside and outside the centre, but it is surprising how little real care of employees is taken by many managers. The computer services manager should be chosen as much for his power of leadership as for his technical ability. Together with the security manager he must take positive steps to secure his centre—quite apart from essentially negative physical and personnel measures. They should endeavour to establish a working climate in which honesty and loyalty are natural and easier than their converses. This is not so difficult as it sounds. There is a fundamental goodness in human nature just as there is a vulnerability to temptation. Both result from a combination of incentives and deterrence.

An example of this not applicable to computers but capable of adaptation and illustration of the theme is a series of notices for customers in a foreign supermarket at intervals on the route out towards the cashiers. The first says words to the effect:

It is so easy inadvertently to put goods into one's handbag or pocket and forget to declare them to the cashier. Please check most carefully to help us keep this shop a pleasant place.
The second:
Just make absolutely sure—please.
The third:

The security of this store is closely supervised in everybody's interests by expert store detectives and closed-circuit television monitors, and please don't forget that each article you buy has to be desensitised by the cashier or a loud alarm is given.

The great object is of course to prevent crime and it must not be forgotten that it takes two to make a theft—the owner and the thief. Who is the more guilty, the seller who tempts with all the power of modern display and fails to make stealing difficult, or the thief? There is at least a joint responsibility.

.   .   .   .   .

One views with mixed feelings the fact that a computer fraternity has grown up among senior computer personnel which permits, no doubt with the highest motives, the borrowing and lending among themselves of equipment, special stationery and know-how. It is said that they even exchange computer time to cover deficiencies in excess program testing times, or abortive run times, and thus avoid management scrutiny and sometimes financial control. This could be a serious risk, and might negate the value of a computer élite. This should certainly be considered as a *raison d'être* of the following chapter on surveillance and must be taken account of in risk management (*see chapter 7*).

CHAPTER 6

Surveillance of People and Property

If physical and electronic controls and personnel security measures have failed to deny access to the criminal or the criminally inclined, (and there will sometimes be a Philby in the best laid schemes) all is not lost. There remains surveillance, which in some aspects is the most distasteful of all security measures. It can be aural or visual and open or secret, offensive or defensive, and be carried out with or without the aid of technology. When done secretly it is espionage or counter-espionage, with all the implications of these arts.

In the authoritative book *Security Administration*[1], surveillance is defined as closely watching, supervising, or guarding, and may be used to effect the security of people, processes or property. Its tools are mainly the senses of hearing and vision, which today are often reinforced and extended by electronic, mechanical and optical techniques.

With one exception, the remaining senses of taste, smell and touch are not used in modern security. Originally the senses did have a security purpose. The sense of taste enabled man to distinguish food which would keep him alive. Smell can reveal the presence of other men, or of animals, or their traces, such as camp fires. Guerillas in the jungles of Malaya and elsewhere used primitive tribes such as the Sakai to provide early warning of the approach of British troops during the emergency. It was said that Sakai, in favourable conditions, could smell cigarettes ten miles away. As recently as the Great War of 1914–18, wires were connected to sentries' arms; the slightest pressure would tell the sentry that someone or some animal was crossing a certain line.

The main exception is that friend of man, the dog, who can detect the presence of man or other animals at considerable distance, and can be trained to find explosives and narcotics whether carried on

[1] See page 115.

the person, concealed in buildings, or buried. It is commonly supposed that this ability is wholly due to the dog's sense of smell, but there is reason to doubt this. If we are to take full security advantage of this uncanny ability of the dog, deep research should be carried out. It may be that we should discover the existence and nature, in dogs at any rate, of the at present mythical sixth sense.

.   .   .   .   .

There are two types of surveillance of concern to management: that arranged by itself to protect the company, and that carried out by a hostile organisation. The first is normally open and the second always secret.

Management Surveillance and Privacy

Whatever one may think of the ethics of surveillance of one's own staff and work-force, there is little doubt that the knowledge that it is being carried out is a powerful deterrent. At the same time, if the need for it is not established in the minds of those affected, it might be so deeply resented as to do more harm than good. Highly-trained staff might leave in dudgeon, there might be hostile press comment and strikes; the company's image might become so tarnished as to affect its trading.

In his address to the Council of Europe in 1970 entitled *Some Threats of Technology to Privacy*, Professor R. V. Jones said, 'The life of the individual in a society has to strike a balance between freedom and discipline. Too little freedom will strangle the individual initiative on which so much of the advance of society depends; excessive freedom, such as the right to drive an automobile on which-ever side of the road as one may from moment to moment choose can result in disaster. It is therefore inevitable that in any society there must be a degree of control or regulation, and this control depends in the first place on information regarding the past, present and predicted behaviour of the system. The state is thus naturally interes-ted in obtaining this information, even at times at the risk of inter-fering with individual privacy, and it happens that because of the recognised need of states to protect themselves against espionage and subversion, there is a rapidly developing technology of both espionage and counter-espionage that can be adapted by any state for the surveillance of its own nationals, and indeed by any organisation for gathering information about its rivals.'

Privacy has been defined as 'the claim of individuals, groups or institutions to determine for themselves when, how and to what extent information about them is communicated to others'[2].

It is clear that some state intrusion into individual privacy is necessary for its protection. The degree varies from country to country, but in Britain and the USA especially there is a number of safeguards for the individual built into their systems. It can be said that prior to arrival of computer and eavesdropping technology, the balance in both countries was about right, but now new and serious problems are posed.

In the first place, intrusion into individual privacy has become very easy. Secondly, the private information of both governments and corporations has become highly concentrated and therefore highly vulnerable to intrusion. We are not here directly concerned with the behaviour of the state. The question relevant to this enquiry is, how far should the corporation be permitted to intrude into individual privacy to safeguard the privacy of its own computer complex?

There is no previous experience on which to rely, and the following principle is therefore a postulate:

The corporate body owning a computer complex to which a general threat exists should limit itself to open surveillance; secret surveillance should only be permitted where a specific threat has been described, or is reasonably suspected.

The situation is perhaps analogous to that of the police use of the breathalyser. They should not use it until they have reason to suspect that something is wrong. Obviously such a policy cannot be forced upon a corporation, since it is no offence to collect information about one's staff or workpeople, although some of the means which can be used may be offensive; e.g., corruption, trespass. If covert or secret methods of surveillance are used, they are bound eventually to become known, and it would be surprising if there was not a consequential loss of morale. If, on the other hand, the surveillance method as explained is obvious and the same for everybody, staff, understanding the need for it, can accept it. And acceptance by those whom it affects is a prerequisite of success in security.

The nub of the argument, therefore, is that to safeguard computers constant open surveillance of the centre, its surrounds and its people

[2] Professor A. F. Westin.

while there, is justified. Secret surveillance of people (as opposed to property) is justified only to cope with a specific threat, and it should be so limited; this principle should also be applied to surveillance of lavatories, changing rooms and places of relaxation.

The methods available to management for open surveillance may be classified as follows:

Watching with the naked eye. This is supervision in its simplest form. For operating convenience as well as security, keeps within computer centres should be partitioned with transparent glass. The point has already been made that outer walls should be opaque. It should be borne in mind that transparent partitioning also permits illegal surveillance. A spy in one keep may be able to observe what is happening in another. With the aid of special contact lenses, telescopic vision can be obtained without it being obvious. This could be prevented or made more difficult by split levels, partial opaqueness or partitions, and careful arrangement of equipment and working tables and desks. At the same time, the security monitoring centre[3] can be centrally placed and raised so that all activities are visible. In a large area the naked eye will be insufficient on grounds of distance alone, and moreover there will be dark corners and dead ground. The cavity beneath the floor, which is inevitable in a computer centre, is also vulnerable.

Watching by optical and electronic means. Persons being watched with the naked eye are usually aware of the fact, but when closed-circuit television or one-way mirrors or long-range telescopes are employed they may not be aware of when they are being surveyed, although they may know that they can be. In these days of miniaturisation, however, it is possible to carry out optical surveillance clandestinely. In the United States, and undoubtedly elsewhere, miniature television cameras have been developed; although they do not give good definition, they can provide a useful record of personal activities. These means can be used openly to cover dark corners and concealed cavities, plant rooms and so on.

Eavesdropping. This expressive word, which stems from the activities of the spy who secretly listened to conversations in the house or in the office by standing under the eaves, has acquired a new significance since the development of the miniature microphone and transmitter.

[3] See page 52.

The modern eavesdropper may listen at a safe distance on an appro-priate radio receiver, or he may prefer to avoid the possible detection of radio transmissions by directly recording on tape in his subject's premises. Here we are concerned with the open possibilities for management monitoring. Some people may be shocked at the very idea, but it is happening all the time. Many conferences are openly tape-recorded, as are press interviews (not always openly, especially press interviews conducted over the telephone).

Further details of the technical devices available for secret watching and listening are given later in the chapter.

.   .   .   .   .

Intruder Surveillance

So far we have been concerned with open surveillance of authorised staff during working hours. At night or at weekends, however, it may be that the centre is unoccupied or lightly manned. If this is so, then a different kind of surveillance would have to be exercised. Intruder alarms to give early warning of illegal entry (including authorised staff at unauthorised times), or attempts at illegal entry, will need to be linked to an appropriate centre such as a police station or works guardroom, or commercial central alarm station, so that force may be sent to the threatened point. If there is a nearby guardroom, it may also be possible to use closed circuit television to confirm or identify the precise point of intrusion.

Burglar alarm systems have to be designed for the particular problem, and it is therefore only possible to generalise here about their nature and capability. They make use of a change in ambient conditions caused by an intruder to trigger an alerting device; change of pressure in a room, change of temperature, change in the pattern of sound or light waves, can all be used to produce a visible or audible warning. The four most important considerations governing the use of burglar alarms are:

(1) *The alarm must occur as early as possible.* Clearly, burglar alarms themselves are not an obstacle. Their business is to detect an illegal intrusion and summon a force to deal with it. The purpose of barriers is to delay the intrusion for as long as possible, and certainly until that force arrives.

Therefore the earlier the alarm can be given in the assault, the more effective will be the barrier and the more sure it is that the help will arrive in time.

(2) *There must be an efficient response.* An alarm system must be linked to guards or police so that action can be taken to deal with the illegal intruder. Preferably the alerting device should not also warn the intruder, since it is obviously better to catch him than frighten him away.

(3) *There should be depth to the burglar alarm system.* It is not unreasonable to suppose that criminals have some technical ability. Certainly old-fashioned burglar alarms have been successfully bridged out by criminals in the past. Today's systems are much more sophisticated, but nevertheless considerable additional security is given by a second layer of independent alarms to give depth to the defences. Defence is always better if that which defends is itself defended.

(4) *False alarms.* The bugbear of alarms is that, due to their necessary sensitivity, carelessness on the part of the owner, failures of landlines and technical faults, they are prone to false alarms. The situation has been sufficiently serious to have given rise to doubts as to whether the false alarm rate of a greatly expanding industry might in the future exceed the police response capability. Happily much is currently being done to reduce the false rate by assault on all its causes. Prospective purchasers of alarms may find it advantageous to employ security companies who are members of the British Security Industry Association[4], which is recognised by the Home Office and the Associations of Chief Police Officers of England, Wales and Scotland as endeavouring to promote high standards. Of especial importance in the alarm field is the certificate of competence issued by the National Supervisory Council for Intruder Alarms Limited[5] to companies which conform to British Standard no. 4737, a main purpose of which is to reduce the rate of false alarms.

[4] See footnote on page 113.
[5] An independent organisation which maintains a roll of approved installers. Further information can be obtained from the director-general, NSCIA, 11 Catherine Place, London, S.W.1.

An excellent account of burglar alarms is given by Gordon Hasler in his book *Integrated Alarm Systems*[6].

We have dealt with open surveillance of staff while working and surveillance of the centre when occupied and unoccupied. We have not yet dealt with surveillance of staff when not working, nor with the secret surveillance and the interrelated subject of hostile surveillance.

Private Lives

It is often said that what staff do off-duty is no business of the employer, and in theory this is true. Yet throughout the ages it has been accepted that the way a person handles his private responsibilities and conducts his private life may have a bearing on their fitness for public responsibility. It was for this reason that for many years divorce was considered to be a bar to public office. While there are no doubt many exceptions, experience has shown that those whose private lives are irregular in the sex sense, or who gamble unwisely or drink too deeply, may become security risks. They may be tempted by women spies, or their gambling and drinking may lead them into debt. Then they can be blackmailed. They may be tempted to make use of their position and power to pay off their debts.

The following story, which has been altered and adapted so as not to reveal the identities of the persons concerned, but which is true in all material respects, illustrates this point.

The executive chairman of a certain major company consulted a security expert about a leakage of information. He had conclusive evidence that the leakage could only be through one of his three most trusted colleagues, the managing director, the financial director, or the technical director. Delicate and detailed enquiries revealed a time pattern of dealing in the company's shares which had resulted in considerable capital gains to a nominee company; but this evidence was inconclusive.

It was recommended that the next area of enquiry should be the private lives of the other directors. The chairman said that he had always made a point of not being interested in or even aware of the private lives of his colleagues. However, he eventually agreed and the most superficial enquiries showed that the financial director had

[6] See page 114.

an irregular private life. The expense of this was an important incentive in his decision to use his privileged position for gambling on the Stock Exchange. His knowledge reduced the element of gamble so far as his company's stocks and shares were concerned, and the gamble became one with his position on the board—a gamble which he subsequently lost.

It is not suggested that every person who leads an irregular sex life, who is in debt, or is an alcoholic, is unreliable in the security sense. Nevertheless, such are predisposing conditions. The inevitable conclusion is that the private lives of employees of computer centres are relevant factors in their loyalty. It is not suggested that spying into their private lives is necessary, except in extreme cases, but that social involvement, that is, the establishment of a social background to the company's activities, is a useful means of getting to know the whole man or woman and their families. In this way, too, early warning of disaffection may be received; if it is early enough, a helping hand may save the person as well as the company.

Prevention is always the first and highest security aim.

.   .   .   .   .

Secret Surveillance

It has been suggested earlier in this chapter that management is only justified in initiating secret surveillance if a need has been demonstrated. This need can range from a reasonable suspicion based on information, which by itself is not conclusive, to the discovery that a member of the computer staff is removing punched cards without authority or obtaining duplicates of computer print-outs. If so, it might be very short-sighted to take immediate punitive action.

If the culprit is an agent of another firm, a turning operation might be far more profitable than mere dismissal or prosecution (turning is the art of persuading someone else's secret agent to change his loyalty and act for oneself). If he does not know he has been discovered, secret surveillance might reveal much more than a one-man operation; for example, a major conspiracy by a rival firm.

In either case, a 'deception' operation becomes a possibility. For example, true information that does not matter could be fed through the agent to his principals to establish credibility, followed by a few selected falsehoods which mattered very much indeed. But many delicate considerations arise. Should the police be informed? What is the legal position in regard to turning or deception, especially if incentives are offered? Should a private investigator be called in?

The police are in a difficult position and a very different one from that of management. Some police officers might decide, and have in similar cases decided, to arrest the immediate agent and thus demolish the chance of turning the tables. In strict law they might be right; from the point of view of management, all chance of retribution or recovery may be thus destroyed. The resultant damage to the firm may be fatal, and there may be a grave loss to the economy; such considerations are inevitably only of indirect interest to the police, and they must not be blamed for this. But the law and usage give the police some discretion in these matters, and this merely enhances the importance of the second basic computer security principle[7]. The police are essentially human and quite capable of the Nelson touch in appropriate circumstances.

It may, however, be necessary to call in a private investigator. Some managers may throw up their hands in horror at this suggestion, but that is a mistaken reaction. Quite apart from Sherlock Holmes, much valuable work has been done by the private investigator. It is true that there are some whose methods and reputations leave much to be desired. A generally recognised professional body, the Association of British Investigators, has made great efforts to establish and maintain a respectable profession, and membership of ABI can be regarded as evidence of probity and integrity.

.   .   .   .   .

The following paragraphs describe briefly the means by which secret surveillance can be carried out (1) against a member of the computer staff by his management acting on information, or (2) against a given management by hostile persons or organisations.

These operations are counter-espionage and espionage, respectively. Since there is often considerable confusion about the meanings of these terms (counter-espionage, for example, is often confused with security), it is necessary to define them.

Espionage is the art and practice of spying to gain secret information. *Counter-espionage* is the art and practice of spying to detect and defeat espionage.

[7] See page 34.

The means by which espionage and counter-espionage are carried out divide into two categories: those which are primarily of human agency, and those which are primarily of technical agency.

Before considering either the human or technical agencies, it is necessary to discuss briefly the motivations of industrial espionage. These are:

(1) *Industrial competition.* Rival companies may be seeking information in connection with the following:

> research and development;
> marketing plans;
> tenders;
> mergers;
> head-hunting.

The competitors seeking such information may be domestic or foreign and, if the latter, they may be aided by their national intelligence agencies.

(2) *Individuals*, for personal gain or for revenge.

(3) *Student and labour force agencies*, for subversive political purposes.

(4) *Hostile foreign powers*, for political, military and industrial purposes, (a) to strengthen industrial potential for war or for effectiveness of foreign policy; (b) to strengthen its own economy and weaken that of its victim. It should be borne in mind that in communist countries all industry is state-owned; industrial espionage is therefore usually carried out by a department of state intelligence.

·   ·   ·   ·   ·

It is useful for defence purposes to classify the means of intrusion into privacy as human or technical, since each method requires different counter-measures. But this might be misleading as the human agency (the spy) will often, if not always, make use of technology to improve his efficiency. Similarly, where the intrusion is technical—a bugging device, for example—it will have have been placed in position by and is, of course, designed to inform a human agency.

There are variations on these themes. For example, some spying devices such as the long-range microphone or telescope do not involve physical intrusion, and the human spy may not be operating actually in the target area, but in an adjacent one. It is therefore convenient to classify them as has been done below.

Primarily human agency. The spy in the computer centre may use technical aids, e.g., cameras, but essentially he relies on his wits and his position as a trusted servant of the company for the information he needs.

The human spy may be of the following types:

(1) A previously trustworthy employee who, for one reason or another, has gone sour of his own free will. Usually there are warning signs. A chip-on-shoulder attitude resulting from promotion disappointment, a feeling of failure, real or imaginary, a nagging or greedy wife, are the commonest predisposing causes of disloyalty and should always be investigated.

(2) One who has been induced by blackmail, extortion, bribery, to work for the hostile agency.

(3) A long-term penetration. In other words, a man or woman who has been hired by a hostile agency, specially trained for the job and infiltrated into the victim organisation through ordinary employment channels.

The behavioural characteristics by which the spy may sometimes be identified include:

(1) Lack of real friends—because of lack of time to cultivate them, and fear that intimate friends would discover the double life.

(2) Exceptional ability at the job. This is an essential quality for spies. Without it, they are unlikely to graduate to key positions.

(3) Lack of hobbies—because of lack of time to develop them.

(4) Quiet, reserved and generally introverted. This is really the security barrier which the spy must have.

(5) Inconspicuousness. Flamboyant people are seldom chosen as spies because they attract too much attention.

It must, however, be strongly emphasised that not all persons displaying these symptoms are or are likely to become spies.

If there are grounds for suspicion, certain tests may be applied. The employee may be moved without warning to other employment. If he or she is a spy, his activities will be dislocated and there will be no time or opportunity to make alternative arrangements. The shock or surprise may make him careless. He may protest too much, or too little.

A case in point is that of Judith Coplon, a young American political analyst who worked in the Department of Justice. She was also a communist sympathiser feeding a Russian espionage network. In 1949 she was convicted and sentenced to a long term of imprisonment. According to Ronald Seth[8],

> 'Towards the end of 1948 . . . the FBI learned that the contents of some of their papers were reaching Moscow. A thorough investigation was instituted, and one by one all possible channels of leakage were eliminated until suspicion came to rest on Judith Coplon. But it was still only suspicion. There was no proof. However, the Department of Justice could run no risk of her seeing and handling any further secret papers, and she was transferred to another division. When she learned of the transfer, according to her chief, "she was very much disturbed". It was on account of these loud protests that the FBI were convinced that she was their quarry.'

It is in circumstances such as this, when there is a definite suspicion that a spy exists, that counter-espionage is justified. The police may be willing to carry this out, a security consultant or a private investigator may be employed, or the management may do it themselves. It should be borne in mind that counter-espionage is a highly specialised technique, and that immense damage can be done by amateurs or through the use of hastily organised or ill-considered procedures.

Primarily technical agency.   In this case the primary means by which management or the hostile force carries out its surveillance is technical, that is to say, the immediate presence instead of being human is a piece or pieces of technical equipment. What follows is largely a summary of relevant parts of R. V. Jones's paper[9].

Mechanical devices.   These on the whole are capable of providing only very limited information. Vibrations caused by movement will reveal the presence of a person, as can the tilt of a building caused by a man's weight moving from one room to another.

[8] See page 116.
[9] See page 114.

Thermal devices. It is possible to detect humans, motor-cars, ships and aircraft by the heat they radiate. Even pictures of a scene can be produced in which the hotter objects show up more brightly than the cooler ones. For example, the exposed portions of the body radiate more heat than those that are clothed, and thus show up as 'whiter'. But although the sensitivity of the thermal detector can be made so great that a surface that is one-thousandth of a degree Centigrade above its surroundings will show up, the amount of information that can be obtained of or by an intrusion of this nature is very limited.

Optical devices. Provided the view is not obstructed, photographs of human beings, equipment and documents can be taken from a long range. It would be possible to record legible letters of about 1 cm. high at a range of 1 km. in good conditions. Where conditions are not favourable, or the view is obstructed, and provided access can be obtained, it is possible to use a miniature camera *in situ*. This can be installed and concealed and set to take photographs at pre-determined intervals by remote control. The one-way mirror is another optical device for seeing without being seen. This has been used by psychologists for demonstrating patients to their students, and reputedly by some industrial firms for observing candidates at interviews.

Reference has already been made to small television cameras and their limited value for secret surveillance. With larger cameras, however, there have been developments which enable the user to see clearly with no more light than is available on an overcast moonless night. Such devices are already used for military purposes.

Counter-measures to defeat optical intrusion are, in the first place, based upon control of access to prevent their introduction into the vulnerable area. Secondly, measures must be taken to prevent remote seeing. Curtains over, or even absence of, windows, bare walls without mirrors or pictures, are advisable. Television receivers should not be permitted in the vulnerable areas. The best way of hiding a pebble is to put it on the beach; a television eye could be placed in a domestic television receiver and appear to be associated with it. This might be traced through its batteries or connections to the electric main direct, otherwise it would only be operating when the television receiver was switched on.

Acoustic devices. These have so far been the most important way of

F

obtaining information from unsuspecting subjects. The microphone has become, and will probably remain, the major technical weapon of espionage and security services, the private enquiry agent, and the industrial spy, since miniaturisation became possible. The miniature microphone has been concealed in many different places ranging from flowers to sugar lumps. It can transmit to a nearby receiver by radio, or can be associated with a telephone.

The easiest way of tapping a telephone is to do so at the subject's terminal. Once the telephone line leaves the apartment, it is more difficult, but it can be done provided the tapper can locate the correct line, which he can do if he gains access to the main junction box. The most spectacular example of this activity was the tunnel device used by Western intelligence agencies under the West–East Berlin frontier to tap Russian military telephones.

Of the several devices which can be used for telephone tapping, the most remarkable is the 'harmonica bug'. Once this is installed in the telephone of the victim, the eavesdropper, who can be anywhere—even thousands of miles away, provided that he is on a direct dialling system—merely dials the victim's number and blows a pre-determined musical note on a harmonica. This note is picked up by the device in the victim's telephone and prevents it from ringing. At the same time, it connects the telephone microphone into the line so that the eavesdropper can listen to any conversation that is taking place within earshot of the victim's telephone.

Once again, countermeasures rely in the first place on control of access to sensitive areas. Since voices can be detected by means of vibrations through windows, doors and walls, particular attention has also to be paid to the vicinity. Special electronic means for detecting concealed microphones have been developed and are in use. If possible, telephones should be excluded from sensitive areas. In a computer centre, for example, telephones could be confined to an external office. This will become the more important if and when telephones are widely developed to provide vision as well as sound.

The laser. A recent development of the laser for eavesdropping is to observe the movement of a surface that is already in the victim's room, and which may be set into vibration by speech, e.g., a calendar hanging on a wall. With certain ancillary devices a microphone can be created in which the calendar acts as a diaphragm.

When all is said and done, surveillance is not a pleasant process. Even in its open form, it can be an intrusion into privacy. In its secret form it may be illegal, especially if bugging equipment is used; it is an offence under the Wireless Telegraphy Act to make a radio transmission without a Post Office licence, and this is true even if the bugging is defensive. If two or more persons are involved and there is any form of corruption, a charge of conspiracy may be sustained, as it was in the Hall and Merken case[10].

In the present mass criminal society it is doubtful if purely defensive operations will always be sufficient, as the following story illustrates.

The powerful British insurance industry, for so long apparently immune to the worst commercial buffets, is becoming increasingly concerned about the erosion of its profits by crime. The latest form of this is a series of systematic fraudulent claims; it is thought that some crooked claimants have made personal fortunes of millions of pounds. It is believed that organised gangs, including some of Britain's most violent criminals, have set fire to buildings by pre-arrangement. Intimidation of witnesses and threats of physical violence are alleged to have been used to ensure the 'cooperation' of insurance company directors, loss adjustors, and members of the London Salvage Corps[11]. The insurance companies complained that because of intimidation or fear they lacked sufficient evidence for a court, and that the police were apathetic.

At any rate, three leaders of the insurance industry were sufficiently worried to have mounted a private undercover operation and to have paid for electronic devices to bug the offices of a suspect claimant[12].

It is to be doubted if the police were apathetic. It is much more likely that their resources were too limited. But even if these resources were substantially increased, it is doubtful whether the police could undertake on any scale counter-espionage operations on private property. They have no power to police private property, only to enter it in special circumstances; yet the private area is growing in size and complexity with every advance of industry and technology.

In a society that shows every sign of a deepening corruption, and meets this with an ever-weakening penology and legal procedures

[10] Lincoln Assizes, 11 Oct 1971. See also page 80.
[11] An organisation maintained by insurance companies covering Greater London and parts of adjacent counties. Its principal task is to provide a follow-up service to the fire brigades.
[12] *The Times,* 6th January 1972.

that were favouring the accused even before intimidation of witnesses became fashionable, the police already have enough problems in the public sector.

It is against this general background that the need for surveillance of computers and people, both open and secret, must be considered by industry and others concerned who have the primary responsibility and maximum incentive for protection of their computers.

Electronic Sweeping

It may one day be possible by electronic or other means to discover the contents of the human mind: its previous experience, its present thinking, and its future intentions. No doubt defensive measures to prevent such detection will also be discovered.

In the meantime, there is available highly specialised and very expensive electronic equipment for the detection or neutralisation of most electronic surveillance devices. The great problem, given the accuracy of the detection devices, is that they only show the condition of a given room at the time they are used. A typical room might cost £100 to 'sweep', as the technical experts call it, and it may not be enough to sweep the room before a conference, because the eavesdropping device may inadvertently be brought into the room by a person authorised to attend.

Nevertheless, in certain circumstances it may be advisable to test from time to time whether unauthorised eavesdropping devices have been placed in the computer centre and elsewhere. There are very few firms who have the necessary equipment, and it is always as well to remember the old intelligence adage that there are no spies, only double spies. Therefore the greatest care in selection must be exercised, and this is best left to the firm's security consultant.

Surveillance and the Law

The selling of information is not a crime in British law. The basis for this is that there is no legal property in an idea. It cannot be patented, registered or stolen, but in the United States the stealing of information has become sufficient of a menace for most of the states to have passed laws aimed at penalising the unauthorised acquisition of information, and there have been some moves in Britain to enact similar legislation. Yet it is not always desirable that information, when stored in a computer or associated data bank, or in a man's head, should be protected.

If over-enthusiastic security officers are let loose on industrial information, they may stultify all progress, an enormous amount of which must come from the free exchange of ideas. Over-securing might create an actual need for industrial espionage, and it would be quite wrong in a number of cases for the press to be denied access to private information. The private lives of public men and women should in many cases be exposed to the public gaze. Part of the punishment of the criminal is the publicity attendant upon his crime.

It might be very difficult to prepare a law which struck a fine balance between individual rights of privacy and the public interest, and indeed this was one of the reasons why the Right of Privacy Bill, which was introduced to Parliament in 1967 by Mr. Alexander Lyon, MP, was defeated on the second reading.

In another attempt to protect the privacy of the individual, and indeed of management, Sir Edward Boyle, Bt., MP, presented the Industrial Information Bill to Parliament in 1968 and it showed up another snag in that, in giving rights of privacy, exceptions had to be made in respect of police investigations, and it also permitted 'investigation undertaken with ministerial authority' and 'investigation in the interests of national security'. No doubt if it had become law other exceptions would have had to be made, and this is one of the troubles of legislating in this delicate private area; that in trying to protect privacy one creates legal rights to intrude upon it.

Should there be a right of eavesdropping? A perfectly good case could be made out for eavesdropping—electronic or otherwise—by the ordinary citizen. There are cases in which the police are either unwilling or unable to carry out investigations, even though a grievous wrong may have been done to an individual. This is the reason for the existence of the civil law and the right of the individual (or a company) to prosecute under the criminal law if he considers a wrong has been done to him. Should he be denied any of the means of investigation which are open to the police in defence of his rights? Certainly some insurance officials have definite views on this matter[13].

Some *Times* reporters secretly recorded conversations of some Scotland Yard detectives which resulted in their prosecution and conviction, and this itself is a form of bugging.

[13] See page 77.

Is the present law adequate?   As has been said, there is no crime of stealing information, but some of the acts which accompany the taking of information may themselves be offensive. The Prevention of Corruption Act, 1906, has been used in several cases, notably that of Elizabeth Hall and Peter Merken[14], who in 1971 were fined under this act having been convicted of conspiracy. The use of this act, of course, is a somewhat blunt instrument for getting a heavier penalty.

Under this act, any person who corrupts one's staff may be prosecuted, and so, too, may the staff who have been corrupted, but the spy who walks in and helps himself to the information cannot be caught under this act, although under the Theft Act of 1968 he might be charged with stealing the sheet of paper on which the information was written.

It seems strange that the Theft Act so recently drafted did not take some account of the theft of information possibility. Indeed, there is one school of thought which considers that it could be used, for in its definition of 'property' it includes 'money and all other property, real or personal, including things in action and other intangible property'.

It can be argued that intellectual property might fall within the term 'other intangible property'. One must suppose that the police legal authorities do not agree with this view, since there has not been a test case, although there has been opportunity.

It may be that there should be some new legislation, but it is to be hoped that it will be aimed more at the actions of the spy and the act of espionage than as an attempt to create privacy. Privacy, surely, like happiness, is an abstract and amorphous idea depending on the behaviour of individuals towards each other. It is up to management to protect its information, which it can do quite well if it has a proper security system based on the notion of risk management[15].

One idea that has been put forward is the setting up of a state watchdog-organisation with powers to receive and investigate complaints of undue intrusion into privacy. If this were developed to include a system of licensing of private detective agencies (which the Association of British Investigators favour[16]), perhaps of security

[14] See footnote on page 77.
[15] See chapter 7.
[16] See page 113.

companies in general (which the British Security Industry Association favour[17]), there might well be sufficient protection for the individual and his privacy, whose boundaries may be better undefined[18].

. . . . .

This does not mean that industrial and commercial management should not protect both its computer and information. They should, and the following chapters show how it can be done. They do not explain computer audit, a technique which is outside the scope of this book but which is closely related to security. The audit trail enables a human check to be made on the scale of about one per cent, which some criminals may consider a reasonable risk. Physical and electronic control of access coupled with an élitist computer profession, and surveillance as described in this chapter, are the real safeguards and they protect against all forms of attack—not merely the lesser dangers such as fraud.

[17] See footnotes on page 58 and page 113.
[18] Since this book went to press the report of the Committee on Privacy (chaired by the Rt. Hon. Sir Kenneth Younger) set up by the government in 1970, has been published. It is in broad agreement with the views expressed in this book. Two other committees are also considering aspects of privacy. One is an interdepartmental committee operating within the British civil service, whose findings may never be published. The other is in USA and operates under Dr. Frances Grommers, a distinguished doctor of medicine. It will report to the Secretary for Health and is known as the Secretary's Advisory Committee on Automated Personnel Data Systems.

CHAPTER 7

Computer Security and Risk Management

There is no possibility whatsoever of achieving the requisite degree of computer security unless the industrial and commercial function of security is understood by top management. As a general truth, management, British, European, American and Japanese, not only fails to understand security, but does not appreciate that it is an industrial function at all. If it had done so, Britain and America might have avoided serious crime waves and their industrial relations might be a great deal better, Japan would not have her pollution problem[1] and, not least of the benefits, the advance towards computerisation would have been slower and surer and less dangerous to society.

.   .   .   .   .

To live and labour in uncertainty is not only the common lot of us all as individuals, but also of corporate enterprise as social units.

Since enterprise exists only in an environment of risk, it is necessary to determine the nature of risk and the ways in which it can be handled. This is the function of risk management in industry and the arrival of the computer is merely another risk factor. It must be stressed at once that risk management is in its infancy and there is a shortage of literature on the subject[2]. The need for it arises, like other branches of the modern managerial art, out of the increasing complexity of industry and its environment.

In primitive times, when man's main possession was his life and his family, he dealt with risk mainly by fighting or by the erection of primitive defences, and, as he acquired property as well, by develop-

[1] Pollution *is* a security problem.
[2] See page 115.

ments of these methods, until the arrival of insurance against crime as a major commercial factor in the early nineteenth century (although fire insurance was well established even in the eighteenth).

Insurance and Increasing Risk

It is perhaps significant that insurance against crime and public policing (the Metropolitan Police Force was founded in 1829) developed *pari passu*. They did so in the conditions (to which they no doubt contributed) of considerable public tranquillity of the Victorian society, with its religious and family disciplines. In these circumstances insurance against insurable business risk was cheap, and until very recently—perhaps ten years ago—often it was far cheaper to insure than to protect.

When losses by crime and fire began to reach alarming proportions in the early 1960s, and to bite into insurance profits, premiums went up; at the same time insurance companies began to demand security as a prerequisite of cover. It was only then that managements thought deeply about security. Before this the security man was often the stoker of boilers and general factotum. Even today, many managements regard security in a negative way. 'How little security can we get away with so as to obtain cover?' managers tend to ask.

Largely as a result of this attitude insurance against fire and theft is becoming difficult to obtain. It is virtually impossible to get cover against pilferage, which now totals more than a million pounds a day.

It was the owner of one of Britain's most famous supermarket chains who said publicly that if he did not lose three to four per cent of his turnover by pilferage, he sacked his display manager. Presumably he budgeted for this loss and indeed this is now common practice. In this way, of course, the customer pays for pilferage, and therefore the cost of living rises. As the thief increases his standard of living without producing, so the customer has to pay more to make up for the stolen article. To do this he needs a rise in wages. It would be interesting to know what percentage of the annual rise in the cost of living is due to increasing dishonesty. Enquiries of various government departments have failed to elicit an answer to the question.

In areas other than pilferage, insurance pressures for tougher security are increasing and the very cost of this is forcing management to face up to the situation.

It has been suggested that another reason why management is at last becoming risk conscious is the upsurge of violence. As a writer[3] in *Security Gazette* cynically observed,

> 'Thin indeed is the crust of an orderly and civilised society. The cries of the weak and the old, the coshed and shot-at ordinary people of this and of other lands have failed to arouse the conscience of those who should lead in the battle against crime. Now that fear of violence and death has reached out into The Establishment itself there may be time to act before our society is destroyed.'

Risk and the Risk Manager's Task

There are two main classes of risk, pure and speculative. Speculative risk depends on the nature of the enterprise; that of a bank is that, being a money-lending institution, it may lend too much money to the wrong people; that of retail selling is whether there are enough customers.

Pure risk is that which arises out of accident or unfriendly actions. These are many and varied and some are peculiar to particular industries. One American book lists more than thirty, ranging from sabotage to falling aircraft! As a generalisation pure risk is insurable and speculative is not.

It is perhaps an oversimplification to say that speculative risk is the responsibility of general management and pure risk of risk management since risk management can be all things to all men. It can take on whatever risk responsibilities general management, as the chief decision-making body of industry and commerce, decides it should; in some enterprises market research, which is concerned to reduce speculative risk, is regarded as a technique of risk management since it can be and often is used as a general intelligence process to discover among other things the present potential and likely future activities of rivals.

Nevertheless, the differentiation is sound for our own and most purposes provided that it is never allowed to become arbitrary. In these terms the risk manager's job is in four parts:

    (1) to list and revise constantly the pure risks to which the business is exposed;

    (2) to eliminate or reduce these risks by organisation and administrative means;

[3] Robert Traini in the December 1970 issue.

(3) to reduce those risks which remain by technical security measures and incentives;

(4) to insure internally or externally against any residual risks.

The relationship between (2), (3) and (4) is a complex interface of economics, social responsibility and availability.

The risk manager must therefore be closely consulted by general management, well informed about general and particular risks, and fully understanding of the techniques of risk reduction and avoidance. His object is to achieve and maintain the security of the enterprise against pure risk. Risk management is the system by which that security is achieved.

The Nature of Security

It is necessary at this stage to make a brief excursion into the philosophy of security so that the nature of the beast may be understood, otherwise false techniques may be developed and used in industry as they have so often been in the external and internal relations of nations. Security is not the antonym of risk; if there were one it would be certainty but there is no such thing. Security has taken many forms through the ages. Castles, banks, trade unions, trade associations, marriage, family life, primogeniture, treaties, were all attempts by man to achieve this desirable and unobtainable state of complete and final certainty.

Paradoxically, any security device which becomes too strong, too powerful, too oppressive, in fact creates its own insecurity. As a large store of money (a form of security) attracts thieves, so does an unsinkable battleship incite the thought and activity to produce a gun which no armour can withstand. Some trade unions of the UK, originally formed to protect the weak worker from the strong boss, are strong enough now to defeat policies of the elected government and may be sowing the seeds of their own destruction. Security that becomes too strong, or even a challenge, is not security at all.

Measures designed to protect information for example, may be so strict as to create a social need for industrial espionage, or even cause that final insecurity, bankruptcy, as the following story of Stardust Inc.[4] (a fictitious American company) illustrates.

[4] First related in *Chemical Engineering* published in USA by McGraw Hill Publishing Co. Inc.

'Once upon a time, there was a dynamic prosperous chemical firm called Stardust Inc., whose executive vice president attended a very disturbing seminar on the "growing problem of industrial espionage and loss of trade secrets". Convinced that Stardust's defences against this sort of loss were inadequate, he proceeded to institute a new protection system. "We must have lost millions from all the know-how that has been leaking out", he told the Executive Committee. "Our new security set-up will stop all that—I'm proud to say it's the most rigorous in the industry, and represents yet another example of Stardust leadership. Sooner or later, you'll see the benefits show up on the balance sheet."

'Well it certainly wasn't "sooner". In fact, the first year after the system was instituted proved to be rather hectic. A couple of key engineers left rather than sign revised secrecy agreements that would have drastically restricted their future employment prospects. A chemist made a mistake deciphering a new super-secret code, and blew up half the laboratory. A colleague of his almost blew up the other half, when he made an uneducated guess rather than go through the red tape of asking for some "confidential" reports that were under lock and key.

'The next years saw improvement in some areas, but new problems in others. A prized Ph.D quit in a huff when he was mildly reprimanded for falling asleep during three successive "Industrial Security" lectures. Another valuable but temperamental researcher left when his name was omitted from the new, streamlined distribution list for certain types of confidential reports; he felt that the omission represented a downgrading of his status.

'A feeling of technical isolation began to set in. Engineers who used to keep Stardust's name before customers and potential employees by giving talks or writing articles, became discouraged by new and more cumbersome procedures for obtaining clearance, and cut down on these activities.

'Also, engineers no longer came back from technical conferences with stimulating ideas. Before going, they had been warned to "keep your ears open but your mouth shut", but people weren't very willing to pour helpful hints into their open ears once it became apparent that Stardust engineers were always taking but never giving.

'Turnover among the technical staff increased. And getting replacements involved costly recruiting campaigns, because applicants no longer flocked to Stardust's doors. (Apparently a rumour had started in the job market that Stardust had lost its glimmer and was bogged down in red tape.)

'As an offshoot of the turnover problem, Stardust felt it had to take legal action against several former employees who had joined a potential competitor in apparent violation of their Stardust contracts. Unfortunately, after considerable legal expense and publicity of the wrong kind, Stardust lost the case when its employment agreements were held to be unreasonably restrictive.

'Stardust also developed other troubles, but the "most rigorous security system in the industry" kept some of these troubles from leaking out. Some years later, therefore, there was considerable surprise in the trade when Stardust, in one of its extremely rare, cautiously worded public announcements, revealed it was filing voluntary bankruptcy papers.'

The word security thus describes a state of balance between risk and certainty. If it is too lenient it may result in anarchy; if it is too strict it becomes a tyranny which provokes forces to overthrow it. To preserve this state of balance is no easier than walking a tightrope in changing ambient conditions.

Risk Management and General Management

It may be asked why risk management needs to be separated from general management. After all, it might be argued, personnel management, which also reaches into all the other functions, is a staff function of general management; why should not risk management be also? The fundamental difference is that risk management is not a subordinate staff function, but a primary operational function on a par status-wise with general management. The reason that they are separate functions is that they require different skills and attitudes. While the general manager must be bold and decisive by nature, the risk manager must be cautious and imaginative.

Fayol's Theory

The need for proper management of risk in industrial enterprises was probably first foreseen by the French industrialist and writer on management, Henri Fayol[5]. He listed the activities of industrial enterprise under six functional headings as follows:

[5] See page 114.

1. Technical: manufacture and production
2. Commercial: marketing
3. Financial: the use and raising of capital
4. Accounting: analysis of costs and stocks, financial
                   statements
5. Managerial: planning and control
6. Security: the safeguarding of property and persons.

Fayol's work on this subject was first produced in 1916 and his identification of the importance of the security function seems to have been many years ahead of his time. Although he did not use the term risk management, he described its function as 'All measures conferring security upon the undertaking and requisite peace of mind upon the personnel'. Fayol's link up of the security of the organisation with the peace of mind of its workpeople has for all practical purposes been ignored by management, and existing bad industrial relations in many industries, which is of course bad for the security of the organisation, is a direct result. Repetitive and boring jobs are not conducive to security, rather the reverse.

There have been many theories of industrial operation since Fayol's but as his was the first (and so far as is known the only one) to embrace the security function, it is convenient to develop the study of risk management by examining in more detail its impact on the other functions. Those who prefer other theories of management can adapt what follows to the theory of their choice.

Manufacture and Production

(a) The protection of technical information from espionage.
(b) The protection of assets from accidental or malicious damage, from theft and pilferage.
(c) The provision of alternative supplies or reserves of materials vital to manufacture.
(d) Continuity of supply of central services such as electricity, gas, water, transport, and communications.
(e) The protection of people from injury.
(f) The provision of loyal labour and its protection from subversion, intimidation, boredom, fear—the 'peace of mind' function. Today we must add protection from terrorism and kidnapping.

All the above concerns of security except (c) extend into other spheres below and it is not proposed to repeat them.

Marketing

The security of marketing and sales is largely concerned with protection of information. Marketing plans for new projects, advertising plans, sales emphasis, mailing lists, particulars of agents and their commissions, are apt to be of high value to competitors and must be protected. Licensing agreements to or from competitors also require security vigilance. Loyalty of sales, sales promotion, and marketing personnel is as important as it is with factory personnel.

Financial

Plans for acquisition or mergers, budgets, subsidiary accounts, plans for raising new capital, can all affect the progress of the company if revealed prematurely to competitors or the press or other unauthorised persons.

Accounting

Almost all the functions of accounting have a security context. One of the main purposes of accounting is to check assets of all kinds. Accounting can be used defensively and offensively to discover and counteract fraud. If it is to function properly a section of it should be investigative. Sometimes this is called or confused with internal audit. The internal auditor is also concerned with checking procedures and looking for economies and from the point of view of the security man, is not necessarily the best person to unearth false records made to conceal fraud. It requires a different type of man to search for fraud and fraudulent intent.

Managerial

The managerial function is more sensitive to bad security than any other area. Management plans are more vulnerable to espionage than any others. One of management's most important functions is the managing of people. People are still the most important asset and the greatest element of risk in business. Their unhappiness, carelessness, malice, disloyalty, and inefficiency, are among the main risks carried by the business—on a par with changes in demand and supply conditions. Management is deeply affected by the environment in which it works but does not control. The impact of the environment on the profitability of the firm is a security calculation. For example, it may be operationally highly desirable to build an oil refinery in a foreign territory near the source of oil. If the local inhabitants or their rulers are likely to be hostile or are unstable, security considerations may rule it out.

It is hoped that the above has demonstrated that the risk manager, like his counterpart in general management, must intrude into all the other spheres (including general management) if he is to be effective. He is a generalist in other people's areas of specialisation, who needs however to be backed up by a team of specialists capable of identifying and evaluating risks.

Risk Managers and Techniques

It hardly needs to be said that the risk manager is a rarity in industry today. There are, however, a number of insurance managers and some of them perform similar functions. But there is a tendency for a manager who is insurance-minded to attempt to generate certainty at prohibitive cost. The task of the risk manager is to reduce risk as far as is humanly possible and then, and then only, to insure. In economic terms 'loss prevention is justifiable to the point where the marginal cost is equal to the marginal saving in loss expectancy. There may be good social reasons for going beyond this point.'[6]

Since management, as a result of the crime wave (for which it has a heavy responsibility) and insurance pressures became aware of the need for security, it has become fashionable to appoint an appropriately-titled executive with a distinguished military or police record as the best way to get rid of a tiresome problem. This philosophy has been responsible to a greater degree than any other managerial activity, or non-activity, for the present bad state of industrial relations, particularly because the 'peace of mind' function has not been understood either by them or their masters. The security, like the personnel function, with which it runs parallel and close, is an inescapable duty of industrial and commercial management. It is no more a police or military function than is police or military management an industrial one. Above all it is a managerial skill.

[6] Dr. R. L. Carter, see page 113.

If this had been realised, the computer would have been introduced in an entirely different way. It is absolutely certain that the whole computer industry, both of Europe and of the United States, lamentably failed to warn industrial management of the immense security problems which would arise from their introduction. This may have been because they themselves had no risk management stream.

Today, the attitude of many computer salesmen to the problem of security leaves much to be desired. But in the end management has only itself to thank for the manifold security problems which the computer has brought and will bring in the future as development increases. If they had studied their craft properly they would have seen the need for risk management and a properly trained risk manager would have quickly evaluated the security risk posed by computers.

The foregoing may at times have seemed to be a digression from the main purpose of the book but unless the need for risk management is realised, there can be no security for computers.

The question which a competent risk manager would have answered about computers and which should still be asked for new or enlarged installations include the following:

(1) What additional risks does the proposed computer installation pose to the security of the company's operation?
(2) What organisational and administrative steps can be taken to reduce or eliminate any of the risks?
(3) What security measures can be employed and what will be their cost?
(4) What additional insurance is necessary and practicable (the espionage risk is uninsurable)?
(5) How does the anticipated cost of security measures compare with the anticipated operational and administrative gains?
(6) Is the residual risk acceptable?

Direction and Organisation

It has been inferred and must now be clearly stated that a risk manager should be given executive powers. These should derive directly from the board and there should be an enabling directive, which might run:

G

To identify, measure and, in conjunction with general management, control risks to the company's assets and the loyalty of its workpeople.

One would expect to see the top level of risk management in the group managing director's office, and similarly at the next level. In some divisions the job might be full-time; in others part-time, or carried out by the divisional general manager himself. In major computer centres the appointment should be full-time and of senior status.

Many risk managers base their work on a check-list, and a series of these designed specially for the computer risk are contained in the following chapter.

CHAPTER 8

Check-lists for the Security of a Company and its Computer Complex

Part 1. The Company

No one security check-list can cover every contingency nor be applicable to every security problem, and the following attempt to codify the teachings of this book is submitted as a guide. It is designed not only for the risk or security manager directly responsible for the computer—indeed, only a part is immediately applicable to him—but as a general as well as a particular view. The importance of corporate responsibility for security cannot be overstressed; if the main board do not form a positive will to secure their enterprise, no amount of ingenuity in a particular sector, no amount of individual effort, nor the finest security equipment in the world, will achieve a reasonable state of security in the vital and vulnerable points.

Having formed a positive will to achieve and maintain the security of the enterprise, the first task of general management is to determine the risk management parameters. If the advice given in the previous chapter is accepted the job will not extend into the speculative sphere, but it cannot, of course, be isolated from decisions taken there. There are also inevitably some fringe areas, as will emerge.

All the activity of the risk manager, and indeed his very existence, depend on the scale and nature of the risk—in other words, the threat. Thus the first task after appointment and fixing of responsibilities is the identification and measuring of the risks. This is often termed assessment of the threat. It is not, of course, possible to measure the various risks in a check-list since their importance and significance will vary according to the type of operation, location and social climate. Thus Table 3 merely lists possible hazards in three categories—those arising from hostile activity, those due to accident, and those which can arise from changing circumstances. The last are categorised separately to stress the fact that the threat assessment or risk identification is a continuous one and not a one-off process. It is not suggested that the list of hazards is exhaustive.

TABLE 1. THE RISK MANAGER AND HIS JOB

Question	*Suggested answers*	*Remarks*
(1) What is the task?	To identify, measure and control by the most economic means risks and threats (a) to the physical and financial (i.e., legal liabilities arising out of defective product, negligence of employees, etc.) assets of the company, (b) to the safety, loyalty, peace of mind of its workpeople, and (c) to the intangible assets of the company such as know-how, information, forward plans	
(2) What type of man does this demand?	Cautious in action, but creative, imaginative, outgoing and sympathetic in thought and behaviour	These are in addition to the other qualities of a good manager
(3) What range of knowledge and experience is required?	(a) Broad managerial experience of the whole enterprise	If it is necessary (and it may often be desirable) to import a risk manager, then his immediate subordinate should be 'homegrown'
	(b) Security theory and practice	At least one commercial company specialises in teaching this.
	(c) Insurance and the insurance market	Chartered Institute of Insurance will assist
	(d) The security industry	
	(e) Sociology, criminology and ecology	Not in depth
	(f) The law, particularly criminal, patent, copyright, fire prevention, safety	

Question	Suggested answers	Remarks
(4) With what skills and techniques should he be familiar?	(a) The making of critical analyses (b) How to carry out inspections (c) The collection, collation and assessment of information (d) Statistical method (e) Electronic data processing	Need not be technical, but must know how to approach a technical subject and to assess technical advice
(5) On what subjects does he need to be continually well informed?	(a) General management's future plans (b) Crime and fire trends (c) Political change affecting the particular industry (d) Industrial relations and trade union attitudes (e) Policies, methods and identities of subversive, revolutionary or other organisations advocating or attempting industrial change not authorised by shareholders or government (f) His company's inputs, products, customers, ultimate consumers (g) The interdependence between group units, customers and suppliers	There must be a board policy which ensures this Wide reading, mixing and viewing The business interruption risk
(6) What adjacent areas and techniques may impinge on his job?	Internal— (a) Personnel department (b) Market research (c) Internal audit (d) Research and development (e) Accounts department	A close relationship between the group personnel officer and the group risk manager is vital to the success of both This, like risk management, depends for its effectiveness on the intelligence process, and there are areas of common interest Part of the purpose of this is to prevent, reveal and discourage fraud Highly vulnerable to industrial espionage The risk manager should ensure that anti-fraud devices such as random stores

Question	Suggested answers	Remarks
		and cash checks are part of the procedure
	(f) Production	Risks arising from dangerous materials and processes
	(g) Sales	Risks associated with customers, sales conditions, methods of distribution
	(h) Legal department	Protection of statutory documents; risks arising from new property acquisitions
	(i) Administration	Including centralised data processing
	External—	
	(j) Police	Especially the crime prevention branch
	(k) Fire brigade	Especially the fire prevention branch
	(l) British Safety Council	See page 113.
	(m) Insurers	

TABLE 2. SECURITY RESPONSIBILITY, COORDINATION
AND COOPERATION

Question	Suggested answers	Remarks
(1) Who is responsible for security		
(a) at main board level?	Managing director	Or any executive member of the main board
(b) executively at group level?	Group risk manager	
(c) at next level?	Risk manager	
(d) of the computer centre?	Computer security manager	Could be called computer risk manager
(2) How is coordination of risk management between	(a) Establishment of technical communications between the various risk and security mangers, coordinated by group risk manager	

Question	Suggested answers	Remarks
group, subsidiaries, divisions, factories and and other sub-units achieved?	(b) Regular meetings	
(3) How is the cooperation of workpeople achieved, especially when the security measures involve inconvenience and intrusion into privacy?	(a) Prior consultation (b) Works and departmental security committees	

TABLE 3. THE GENERAL RISK

Question	Possible answers	Remarks
(1) What risks can arise from hostile action?	Manipulation for illegal power Theft of cash and goods Theft of information Pilferage Fraud Sabotage and malicious damage Arson and malicious ignition Head-hunting and defections Passive sabotage Subversion and penetration of labour force.	Including burglary and robbery Including credit card fraud Including corruption of process This can be of two kinds: internal—withdrawal of own labour, or external, e.g. withdrawal of labour of vital suppliers. Go-slows and work-to-rules are included in this term, as are certain kinds of picketing

Question	*Possible answers*	*Remarks*
	Interception of communications	
	Hi-jacking and freight theft	
	Kidnapping	How much ransom would your board be prepared to pay for, say, its chairman? (The risk is insurable.)
	Armed attack	Revolution and riot are the responsibility of the military or the police, but certain precautions may be advisable
(2) What risk can arise from accident?	Fire Over-heating Flood Frost Hurricane Explosion Power failure Fuel shortage Falling aircraft Danger to life and health from plant and processes Prosecution	
(3) What changes should be examined and anticipated to see whether they pose special and additional risks?	New premises Extension to premises Computerisation, or extension thereof Government legislative proposals Local government plans Competitor advances in products and marketing New products/processes/customers/suppliers	It is especially important that the risk manager be aware in advance of change

It is not relevant here to examine in detail the application of the general risk to any part of the industrial complex other than the computer centre. This is not only a matter of relevance, but of practicability; even companies in the same line of business vary so much that a solution to the security problem of one may be of only limited help to another. But the approach is fairly standard and that begins with determination of the vulnerable points.

Vulnerable points (vps) include:

(1) processes, materials, equipment or information whose loss

or improper use could be disastrous or serious or prejudicial
to the enterprise;

(2) processes, materials, equipment or conditions which are or
might be hazardous to life and health.

When the list of vps has been completed, and this may initially
take many weeks, the next stages are:

their testing against the general risks (see table 3 above) to
establish which are applicable to each particular vp—the
translation of the general into the particular risk;

the measurement of the risk to them as disastrous, serious or
prejudicial;

the application of risk management techniques to the elimination,
reduction and, if necessary, insurance of those particular
risks which remain.

The next part will illustrate this technique in detail in regard to
computers.

Part 2. The Computer Complex

The purpose of this part is to provide a detailed check-list for the
security of a computer complex. It does not include the subject of
safety of people, which is a special science beyond our present scope.
As has been shown it is, however, within the task of the risk manager.

It is, of course, concerned primarily with computers *in situ*. It does
not cover security during manufacture and purchasers of computers
would be well advised to negotiate non-disclosure contracts with the
manufacturer to cover the fidelity of employees involved in the
design and application of their computers.

The table which follows must be read in conjunction with the
following explanatory notes.

(1) It is only a hypothetical case, intended to illustrate and
summarise the theories and recommendations proposed in
earlier chapters.

(2) The risks, classifications and remedies will therefore not be
applicable to all, or even any particular case.

(3) The letters *A*, *B* and *C* are arbitrary classifications of the
degree of harm to the company in the worst case, e.g.,

write-off of equipment, as opposed to damage which can be repaired. In these terms,

A = disastrous
B = serious
C = prejudicial

(4) The check-list and the security suggestions in it are not and cannot be exhaustive. Only the owner and his expert risk manager and security consultant can produce the exhaustive list of the specific rules and practical counter-measures.

The most striking feature of the table is, of course, the manifested importance of control of access. Except for external telecommunications where access is beyond the control of the company, it may and must be applied to all vulnerable points. Secondly, the security of personnel of all grades, whether requiring regular access as staff, or occasional access as visitors or for maintenance, is a common denominator of all security problems.

TABLE 4. THE COMPUTER RISK

Vulnerable Point	General and specific risk	Class	Preventive and remedial action	Page references and remarks
(1) The computer and peripheral equipment (hardware)	(a) Accidental destruction by fire and deliberate destruction or severe damage by fire or violence or neglect or mal-operation	A	Correct design, construction and siting of computer centre	p. 39 et seq
			Control of access and keep system	p. 47 et seq
	Disgruntled workpeople		Filtering, aftercare, welfare and surveillance of personnel, including constant supervision of visiting personnel and service engineers	p. 54 et seq
	Agents of rivals or hostile foreign power			p. 63 et seq
	Politically motivated students		Early warning systems to detect fire, heat, smoke and illegal intrusion	pp. 46 & 67
	Urban guerillas		Local fire extinction and quick communications with fire brigade	p. 45
	Racists, feminists or other extremists		Prior arrangements to buy or borrow time (back-up)	Security arrangements of alternative computers must be satisfactory
	Riots and mob violence		Agreed and rehearsed emergency plans, especially police and fire brigade	

Vulnerable Point	General and specific risk	Class	Preventive and remedial action	Page references and remarks
			Alternative or manual control of processes	
			Duplication of programmes	Duplicates in safe storage—p. 48
			Economic insurance of remaining risk	
			Reduction of dependence if risk residue is unacceptable or insurance unobtainable, e.g., by two smaller computers instead of one big one—these being compatible in all respects	
	(b) Fraud Internal External Combinations	A	Build in quantity limit and controls Control of access and keep system of the central processing unit itself	Including key and switch control
	Via communications		Filterings, aftercare, welfare and surveillance of personnel	p. 54 et seq p. 63 et seq
			Random testing of programmes and other facets of internal audit	
			Anti-collusion and pinning devices	

		Measure	Notes
		Insurance and bonding	
(c) Passive sabotage (internal)	B	Discourage unions, or arrange no-strike, etc., contracts	
Go-slow		Automation of as many essential functions as possible and ensure independent maintenance	
Work-to-rule		Designation and training of alternative staff	Especially if the first action against passive sabotage is not practicable
Strike			
(d) Passive sabotage (external)—denial of vital supplies and services, including by picketing	B	Standby electric power	
		Direct telephone or telex lines	Radio alternatives are sometimes practicable
		Reserve of fuels, lubricants, spare parts, catalysts, tapes, stationery, food and water	
		Reserve transport to bring staff to work	
		Courier system Courier	
(e) Manipulation for illegal power	A	Control of access	If this were part of a national plan of usurpation, then the

Vulnerable Point	General and specific risk	Class	Preventive and remedial action	Page reference and remarks
			Exclusion of subversive or potentially subversive persons from computer staff and work-force and adjacent areas	disaster would be of a national character
	(f) Defections	C	Early warning of unrest	p. 54
			Avoidance of undue dependence	
			Constant watch on morale	
			Publicised salary and promotion procedures	
	(g) Flood and water damage	B	Early warning of rising water, high tides, dam bursts, inclement weather, storms	
			Waterproofing of ceiling	
			Correct siting (no basement installations)	
			Emergency drainage (but this must not provide access)	
	(h) Theft of information (often called industrial espionage)	B	Control of access on the need-to-know basis	p. 42

	Filtering, aftercare, welfare and surveillance of personnel	p. 54 et seq
	Early warning	p. 63 et seq
	Safe storage	p. 48
	Prevention of unauthorised observation, internally and externally	
	Training of personnel in information security	
	Monitoring	
	Clubs	
	Contract of confidentiality with manufacturers	
	Duplicate back-up files or the ability to recreate files	
A	Control of access	
(i) Deception by introduction of false data or wrongful manipulation of programmes	Filtering, aftercare, welfare and surveillance of personnel	
	Internal audit—cipher, coding or check digit systems and *ad hoc* program listings	

Vulnerable Point	General and specific risk	Class	Preventive and remedial action	Page reference and remarks
(2) Data centre (software and data)	(a) Theft of information (input and output data)	B	Control of access to storage centre	p. 42
			Strongroom construction of storage centre	p. 49
			Multiple locking of access points	
			Space and perimeter detection	p. 67
			Filtering, aftercare, welfare, surveillance and searching of personnel	p. 54 et seq p. 63 et seq
			Intelligence system to provide early warning of loss	This need not involve espionage, but does mean a watch on competitors
			System of recording movement of files or programmes—cataloguing	
	(b) Destruction of information	A	Design, construction and siting of storage	
	Flood		Control of access	
	Magnets		Early warning of adverse conditions	
	Fire Overheating Malice or direct violence		Automatic switch-off of power	

	Interference with air-conditioning		Safe storage of source documents and duplicate programs	This might be selective
	Vermin		Effective maintenance of structures and services	
(3) Terminals and VDU	Theft of information and introduction of false data	B	Control of access Monitoring	
			Codes	
			Filtering, aftercare, welfare and surveillance of personnel having access to terminal	
			Internal audit	
			Denial of observation of VDU	
(4) Telecommunications	(a) Interception of computer communications for—eavesdropping, extraction of information introduction of false data	B	Externally, direct line, and categorical assurances about its privacy (except for national security purposes) from Post Office Corporation	Similar considerations arise over the services of computer bureaux
	cryptographic processes		Internally and peripherally, all computer lines should be access-controlled	
	fraud		Supervision of maintenance staff	
			Access codes	

Vulnerable Point	General and specific risk	Class	Preventive and remedial action	Page reference and remarks
	(b) Disruption by deliberate or accidental severance	B	Secure alternative radio, landline and courier service	
	(c) Disruption of normal and emergency com- munications	A		

CHAPTER 9

Subversion by Computer

Many a tyrant has been moved by greed for power, but only in our time has mind control become an applied science, open to many abuses as well as to beneficient uses. Professor James McConnell, a psychologist of Michigan University, once said, 'If I wanted to control the world, I would find ten bright people and, one by one, gain control of their behaviour. Then I'd send each one out to grab ten more. It would take a matter of a year or two to take over, say, the 50 million people of Britain.'

This may or may not be true of our complex human society, with its rich variety of intellects and its tradition of indiscipline, but similar possibilities with the docile computer are real enough.

. . . . .

During the writing of this book a case was reported from California of an information theft by one computer from another. The spying computer took over a computer service bureau terminal, having previously obtained the pass code by electronic interception. The only reason that the crime was detected was that the bureau, in accordance with a previously made arrangement, delivered the punched cards to its customer. The customer denied having ordered these punched cards and they were therefore printed out to discover what error had occurred.

Not the least fascinating part of the case was a report than an excited sergeant of police mistakenly wrote out a charge under Californian state law indicting the computer with the unauthorised acquisition of information from another computer. Perhaps this is a foretaste of things to come.

In the same issue of the journal which reported the case was a good illustration of American marketing vitality. There was an advertisement headed in very bold type, *We have built a computer to protect your computer*. This seems to be good business for the computer industry. First they sell you a computer; then a spy computer to your rival; finally they sell you a security computer. Perhaps somebody should start now to work out the economics of this. We might be better off with our old chief accountant and his hundred clerks.

And this is not all: the rapidity of obsolescence of computers is beginning to look like that of modern motor-cars. Certainly there is evidence that the computer companies are intensifying their sales efforts. Their salesmen are becoming exceptionally well trained and are probably better paid than most others. Certainly they and their technical back-up are very persuasive. They are another stress factor in the life of that already over-stressed person, the computer services manager, who is trying to get his company's hardware to live up to promises he never made. Just as his process, after many months of sweat and toil, is nicely balanced, he hears the knock on the door of the purveyor of the new, improved, super-answer to all his problems. A new generation of computers has been born!

It is no more easy to resist this shiny new monster than the temptation to buy a better motor-car than Jones down the road. Apart from that, there is the fact that the present hardware cannot run for very long without software that is continuously improved and updated. No one wants to update software for an old computer, especially when they are already behind with the software for the new generation. Moreover, good programmers and analysts are hard to find and they naturally tend to gravitate to the newest systems.

From the point of view of the security man, there is little doubt that there will be a constant development of the computer. While the final dimension cannot be foreseen, the general direction of advance is obvious enough. At present computers only compute serially according to information fed into them piece by piece. Advances in design are even now resulting in computers that can mimic the more complex operations of the human brain; from there it may be a short step to the creating by a computer of even more complicated and refined machines of its own design; something perhaps that man himself could neither design, nor comprehend, nor control.

It was pointed out at the beginning of this book that today's computer was 'intellectually a moron and morally permissive'.

What is our situation if the computer becomes intellectually a genius, transcending all human genius, and at the same time remains morally permissive?

Do we not have here the nub of a new and perhaps final problem for the security man, whose art and science, derived from man's main protective instinct, have so far enabled us to go forward and survive in freedom? What if this latest advance could lead to an intellectual takeover by the robots? Perhaps it is the job of the security man to interfere with or advise against development if he considers it prejudicial to the survival of us and our free spirit. Others may argue, as of the breaking of the sound barrier, that once we cease to go forward we shall go backwards. Of course, it all depends on what is meant by progress. Is the invention of plastics, for example, true progress, when one looks at the ecological consequences?

There is one final point: hitherto it has been adjudged that the best way to overthrow a government subversively has been through the trade unions. Lenin himself said:

> 'It is necessary ... to resort to all sorts of stratagems, manoeuvres and illegal methods, to evasions and subterfuge, in order to penetrate the trade unions and to remain in them, carrying on communist activities inside them *at all costs*' (author's italics).

If Lenin were alive today, I do not believe he would alter this statement, but he might add:

> 'The best way of achieving power for the trades unions once they have been penetrated is to ensure that they have access to relevant management and government information, nearly all of which is processed and stored in computer centres. Furthermore, in the future computers will be the main instruments by which political, industrial, economic, military and police power will be exercised.
>
> 'It is therefore necessary to resort to all sorts of stratagems, manoeuvres and illegal methods, to evasions and subterfuges, in order to penetrate the computer complexes and to remain in them, carrying on subversive activities at all costs.'

The picture is not entirely a gloomy one. At least one can say that the advent of the violent protester, the urban guerilla, the militant schoolchild, the frenetic female, the campus incendiary, the highwayman trade unionist, and all the other overturners of the world, has created a bonanza for the security man and the industry which supports him. They must be, and indeed are trying to be, worthy of their calling.

References

ASSOCIATION OF BRITISH INVESTIGATORS
This is a recognised professional body which insists on a high standard of ethics and behaviour for it's members. Further details from the Secretary, A B I, 2 Clements Inn, London W.C.2.

BELSON, Dr. W. A.
Author of a paper entitled *The Extent of Stealing by London Boys and Some of its Origins*. Dr. Belson is head of the Survey Research Centre, London School of Economics, London, W.C.2.

BRITISH SAFETY COUNCIL
The largest industrial safety organisation in Europe, it offers advisory services with the object of improving safety and gaining higher productivity. Further particulars can be obtained from James Tye, Director General, British Safety Council, National Safety Centre, Chancellor's Road, Hammersmith, London, W6 9RF.

BRITISH SECURITY INDUSTRY ASSOCIATION
A trade association representing by volume of business about 90% of the British security industry, with aims to improve the ethics and quality of the service offered by the security industry. Further particulars can be obtained from the Secretaries, BSIA, 36 New Broad Street, London, E.C.2.

CARTER, Dr. R. L.
Dr. Carter is a lecturer in insurance at the University of Nottingham. He has made notable contributions to the science of risk management.

CURRER-BRIGGS, Noel
Author jointly with Brian Kennett and Jane Paterson, of *Handwriting Analysis in Business* published by Associated Business Programmes Ltd. in 1971. He was editor of *Security—Attitudes and Techniques for Management*, published by Hutchinson.

DRUCKER, Peter
American management expert and writer of a number of books on the subject including *The Age of Discontinuity*, published by Heinemann

1969, which forecasts a transition from the industrial society to the knowledge society.

EAST-WEST DIGEST
A fortnightly journal published by the Foreign Affairs Publishing Co. Ltd., 139 Petersham Road, Richmond, Surrey. This journal is a most useful guide to the activities and identities of revolutionary organisations. It is edited by Geoffrey Stewart-Smith, M.P. for Belper.

FAYOL, Henri
Author of a classic work on management first published in 1916, most recently published by Pitman in 1949 under the title of *General and Industrial Management*. So far as is known Fayol was the first management expert to understand the role of security and to see it as a major industrial function.

FIRE PROTECTION ASSOCIATION
This association does research into the causes of fire and provides technical and general advice of all aspects of fire protection. It is largely financed by the insurance companies and Lloyd's. It has important overseas links especially with Belgian and French Fire Protection Associations which brings together fifteen bodies for the purpose of exchanging information and experience. Its literature on fire prevention is unexcelled especially its recent publication *Fire Protection of Computers and Ancillary Equipment* which is obtainable from the FPA, Aldermary House, Queen Street, London, EC4N 1TJ.

HASLER, Gordon
Author of *Integrated Alarm Systems* which is obtainable from Chubb Alarms Ltd., 29 Enford Street, London, W.1. This book is mainly of a technical nature in that it explains the working of alarm systems in some detail. It is also thoroughly readable from the point of view of the layman.

INDUSTRIAL SECURITY
This bimonthly journal is published by the American Society for Industrial Security, 404 NADA building, Washington D.C. 20006, USA. It has a wide circulation among security officers and those involved in security in the United States and Europe particularly. Its authoritative articles cover a wide range of security matters.

JONES, R. V., Professor of Natural Philosophy, Aberdeen University.
His paper entitled *Some Threats of Technology to Privacy* delivered to the Council of Europe, is an outstanding contribution to the subject. Those who took part in the Second World War will remember that it was he who first foresaw and helped to defeat the deadly German device called the Knickebein. A fascinating account of Jones's contribution is given in Churchill's Memoirs, Vol. II pp. 339–42, in which he makes an amusing reference to the de-Knickebeined Luftwaffe.

McCLINTOCK, Dr. F. H. and AVISON, Howard
Joint authors of *The State of Crime in England and Wales,* Heinemann 1969. They concluded from their investigations that on the basis of existing crime in the UK 8% of women and 31% of men will be convicted of a standard list offence at some time in their lives.

NATIONAL SUPERVISORY COUNCIL FOR INTRUDER ALARMS
This is an independent organisation originally financed by the British Security Industry Association for the purpose of policing the intruder alarm industry. It maintains a role of approved installers. Further particulars can be obtained from Rear-Admiral D. Callaghan, Director General, NSCIA Ltd., 11 Catherine Place, London, S.W.1.

PROTECTION
Although not specifically mentioned in the text this journal which is published monthly by Alan Osborne & Associates, 1/113 Blackheath Park, London, S.E.3., is the official journal of the Institution of Industrial Safety Officers. Although primarily concerned with safety it periodically looks at crime and fire prevention, and risk management on a theme of loss prevention as a whole.

RADZINOWICZ, Professor Sir Leon
Wolfson Professor of Criminology, University of Cambridge and Director of the Institute of Criminology. The author of many works on and original contributions to the science of criminology. One of his books, *Ideology and Crime* (Heinemann 1966), illuminates the whole scene of crime and criminals in the present day.

RISK, RISK MANAGEMENT AND INSURANCE
Paper by W. Horrigan, lecturer in insurance in the University of Nottingham, published by Withdean Publications Ltd., 169 Dyke Road, Hove, Sussex. The most useful treatise on a subject which has not been thoroughly explored. Most of chapter 7 of *Computer Security* is based on this paper.

SECURITY ADMINISTRATION
A book by Richard Post and Arthur Kingsbury, published by Charles C. Thomas, Springfield, Illinois. This book is the nearest thing to a security encyclopaedia which has yet been published and gives a most useful perspective as well as up-to-date technical advice.

SECURITY GAZETTE
A monthly journal published by Security Gazette Ltd., 326 St. John Street, London, EC1V 4QD. which although concentrating primarily on crime prevention gives more than adequate coverage of fire and safety management. It is authoritative and highly respected as an independent view of the security scene in the UK.

SECURITY SURVEYOR
A bi-monthly journal published by Victor Green Publications Ltd, 44 Bedford Row, London W.C.1, for the Association of Burglary Insurance Surveyors. This concentrates on security from the viewpoint of the insurance surveyor and includes useful technical information.

SECURITY WORLD
An American monthly publication by Security World Publishing Co. Inc,. 2639 South La Cienega Blvd., Los Angeles, California 90034. It is authoritative, lively, and comprehensive. The publishers also sponsor the International Security Conference which takes place annually in Chicago and elsewhere in the United States. Security World's conferences are unique in their contribution to the science of security.

SETH, Ronald
Author of many books on the subject of espionage particularly the *Anatomy of Spying* (Arthur Barker 1961), and *Unmasked* (Hawthorn, New York, 1965).

TOTAL LOSS CONTROL
This is another name for risk management. There are two publications of note. One is *Total Loss Control* by John A. Fletcher and Hugh M. Douglas published by Associated Business Programmes Ltd., 17 Buckingham Gate, London, S.W.1, in the UK in 1971. This book is useful and has a somewhat different view of risk management but gives rather minimal coverage to crime prevention. Although of recent origin the index does not even mention the computer. *Management Introduction to Total Loss Control* is by James Tye, Director General of the British Safety Council (see above). This is a contribution to the subject with emphasis on the safety aspects.

Index